Canon Barnett

Practicable Socialism

Essays on social reform

Canon Barnett

Practicable Socialism
Essays on social reform

ISBN/EAN: 9783337295806

Printed in Europe, USA, Canada, Australia, Japan

Cover: Foto ©Suzi / pixelio.de

More available books at **www.hansebooks.com**

ESSAYS
ON
SOCIAL REFORM

Crown 8vo, price 5s.

AN INQUIRY INTO SOCIALISM.

By THOMAS KIRKUP,

Author of the Article on 'Socialism' in the 'Encyclopædia Britannica.'

'A very thoughtful and sympathetic study of the modern socialistic movement, with the history of which the author has a very thorough acquaintance.'—CONTEMPORARY REVIEW.

'We have no hesitation in describing this as the clearest statement we have read of the aims and methods of Socialism.'—WESTMINSTER REVIEW.

London: LONGMANS, GREEN, & CO.

PRACTICABLE SOCIALISM

ESSAYS ON SOCIAL REFORM

BY THE
REV. AND MRS. SAMUEL A. BARNETT

LONDON
LONGMANS, GREEN, AND CO.
AND NEW YORK: 15 EAST 16th STREET
1888

INTRODUCTION.

The following Essays have been written at different intervals during our fifteen years' residence in East London. They were written out of the fulness of the moment with a view of giving a voice to some need of which we had become conscious. They do not, therefore, pretend to set forth any system for dealing with the social problem; they are simply the voice of the dumb poor, of whose mind it has been our privilege to get some understanding. They are published now in response to the requests of many to whom they have been some guide in the ways of service, and in the hope that the experience they offer may bring rich and poor together. It will be noticed that two or three great principles underlie all the reforms for which we ask. The equal capacity of all to enjoy the best, the superiority of quiet ways over those of striving and crying, character as the one thing needful are the truths with which we have become familiar, and on these truths we take our stand. Although the Essays do not pretend to form a connected whole, it will be seen that their arrangement is subject to some order. Those placed first set forth the poverty of the poor. Those which follow suggest some means by which such poverty may be met (1) by individual and (2) by united action, with some of the dangers to which charitable effort seems to be liable. As we look back over the experience which these Essays recall, we are conscious of shortcomings and failure, but they are due to our own want of wisdom and of faith, and we still believe that God's will may be done on earth as it is in heaven, and that the doing of His will means at last health and wealth. Each Essay is signed by the writer, but in either case they represent our common thought, as all that has been done represents our common work.

SAMUEL A. BARNETT AND HENRIETTA O. BARNETT.

ST. JUDE'S, WHITECHAPEL: *May* 1888.

CONTENTS.

		PAGE
I.	THE POVERTY OF THE POOR. By Mrs. S. A. BARNETT (July 1886)	1
II.	RELIEF FUNDS AND THE POOR. By REV. S. A. BARNETT (Nov. 1886)	22
III.	PASSIONLESS REFORMERS. By Mrs. S. A. BARNETT (August 1882)	48
IV.	TOWN COUNCILS AND SOCIAL REFORM. By REV. S. A. BARNETT (Nov. 1883)	62
V.	'AT HOME' TO THE POOR. By Mrs. S. A. BARNETT (May 1881)	76
VI.	UNIVERSITY SETTLEMENTS. By REV. S. A. BARNETT (Feb. 1884)	96
VII.	PICTURES FOR THE PEOPLE. By Mrs. S. A. BARNETT (March 1883)	109
VIII.	THE YOUNG WOMEN IN OUR WORKHOUSES. By Mrs. S. A. BARNETT (Aug. 1879)	126
IX.	A PEOPLE'S CHURCH. By REV. S. A. BARNETT (Nov. 1884)	142

		PAGE
X.	CHARITABLE EFFORT. By Mrs. S. A. BARNETT (Feb. 1884)	157
XI.	SENSATIONALISM IN SOCIAL REFORM. By REV. S. A. BARNETT (Feb. 1886)	173
XII.	PRACTICABLE SOCIALISM. By REV. S. A. BARNETT (April 1883)	191
XIII.	THE WORK OF RIGHTEOUSNESS. By REV. S. A. BARNETT (Nov. 1887)	204

PRACTICABLE SOCIALISM.

I.

THE POVERTY OF THE POOR.[1]

Subscribers wishing to purchase Early Second Hand copies of this work are requested to send their names to the Librarian, who will forward particulars of price as soon as the book can be spared for sale.

[1] Reprinted, by permission, from the *National Review* of July 1886.

		PAGE
X.	CHARITABLE EFFORT. By MRS. S. A. BARNETT (Feb. 1884)	157
XI.	SENSATIONALISM IN SOCIAL REFORM. By REV. S. A. BARNETT (Feb. 1886)	173
XII.	PRACTICABLE SOCIALISM. By REV. S. A. BARNETT (April 1883)	191
XIII.	THE WORK OF RIGHTEOUSNESS. By REV. S. A. BARNETT (Nov. 1887)	204

PRACTICABLE SOCIALISM.

I.

THE POVERTY OF THE POOR.[1]

It is useless to imagine that the nation is wealthier because in one column of the newspaper we read an account of a sumptuous ball or of the luxury of a City dinner if in another column there is the story of 'death from starvation.' It is folly, and worse than folly, to say that our nation is religious because we meet her thousands streaming out of the fashionable churches, so long as workhouse schools and institutions are the only homes open to her orphan children and homeless waifs. The nation does not consist of one class only; the nation is the whole, the wealthy and the wise, the poor and the ignorant. Statistics, however flattering, do not tell the whole truth about increased national prosperity, or about progress in development, if there is a pauper class constantly increasing, or a criminal class gaining its recruits from the victims of poverty.

The nation, like the individual, is set in the midst of

[1] Reprinted, by permission, from the *National Review* of July 1886.

many and great dangers, and, after the need of education and religion has been allowed, it will be agreed that all other defences are vain if it be impossible for the men and women and children of our vast city population to reach the normal standard of robustness.

The question then arises, Why cannot and does not each man, woman, and child attain to the normal standard of robustnesss? The answers to this question would depend as much on the answerer as they do in the game of 'Old Soldier.' The teetotallers would reply that drink was the cause, but against this sweeping assertion I should like to give my testimony, and it has been my privilege to live in close friendship and neighbourhood of the working classes for nearly half my life. Much has been said about the drinking habits of the poor, and the rich have too often sheltered themselves from the recognition of the duties which their wealth has imposed on them by the declaration that the poor are unhelpable while they drink as they do. But the working classes, as a rule, do not drink. There are, undoubtedly, thousands of men, and, alas! unhappy women too, who seek the pleasure, or the oblivion, to be obtained by alcohol; but drunkenness is not the rule among the working classes, and, while honouring the work of the teetotallers, who give themselves up to the reclamation of the drunken, I cannot agree with them in their answer to the question. Drink is not the main cause why the national defence to be found in robust health is in such a defective condition.

Land reformers, socialists, co-operators, democrats would, in their turn, each provide an answer to our question; but, if examined, the root of each would be the same—in one word, it is Poverty, and this means scarcity of food.

Let us now go into the kitchen and try and provide, with such knowledge as dietetic science has given us, for a healthily hungry family of eight children and father and mother. We must calculate that the man requires 20 oz. of solid food per day, i.e. 16 oz. of carbonaceous or strength-giving food and 4 oz. of nitrogenous or flesh-forming food. (The army regulations allow 25 oz. a day, and our soldiers are recently declared on high authority to be underfed.) The woman should eat 12 oz. of carbonaceous and 3 oz. of nitrogenous food; though if she is doing much rough, hard work, such as all the cooking, cleaning, washing of a family of eight children necessitate, she would probably need another ounce per day of the flesh-repairing foods. For the children, whose ages may vary from four to thirteen, it would be as well to estimate that they would each require 8 oz. of carbonaceous and 2 oz. of nitrogenous food per day: in all, 92 of carbonaceous and 23 oz. of nitrogenous foods per day.[1]

For the breakfast of the family we will provide oatmeal porridge with a pennyworth of treacle and another pennyworth of tinned milk. For dinner they can have Irish stew, with 1¼ lb. of meat among the ten, a pennyworth of rice, and an addition of twopennyworth of bread to obtain the necessary quantity of strength-giving nutriment. For tea we can manage coffee and bread,

---

[1] To those who have had experience of children's appetites it may seem as if their daily food had been under-estimated. A growing lad of eleven or twelve will often eat more than his mother, but the eight children, being of various ages, will probably eat together about this quantity, and it is better, perhaps, to under- than over-state their requirements.

but with no butter and not even sugar for the children; and yet, simple fare as this is, it will have cost 2*s.* 5*d.* to feed the whole family and to obtain for them a sufficient quantity of strength-giving food, and even at this expenditure they have not been able to get that amount of nitrogenous food which is necessary for the maintenance of robust health.

A little table of exact cost and quantities might not be uninteresting:—

Quantity of Food	Cost	Carbonaceous	Nitrogenous
BREAKFAST—OATMEAL PORRIDGE.	s. d.	oz.	oz.
1¼ lb. Oatmeal . . .	2¼	14	3
1½ pint Tinned Milk .	1½	2¼	1
½ lb. Treacle . . .	1½	7	—
DINNER—IRISH STEW.			
1¼ lb. Meat . . .	8	3½	3½
4 lb. Potatoes . . .	2½	14	2
1¼ lb. Onions . . .	1	5½	1¼
A few Carrots . . .	1	¼	–
½ lb. Rice	1	7	½
1½ lb. Bread . . .	2¼	13½	2¼
TEA—BREAD AND COFFEE.			
2½ lb. Bread . .	3¾	22½	3¾
2½ oz. Coffee . . .	2½	¼	¼
1½ pint Tinned Milk .	1½	2¼	1
Total . . .	2 5	92	18½

But note that the requisite quantities for the whole family are 92 oz. of carbonaceous and 23 oz. of nitrogenous substances.

Another day we might provide them with cocoa and bread for breakfast; lentil soup and toasted cheese for dinner; and rice pudding and bread for tea; but this fare presupposes a certain knowledge of cooking, which but few of the poor possess, as well as an acquaintance with the dietetic properties of food, which, at present, is far removed from even the most intelligent. This day's fare compares favourably with yesterday's meals in the matter of cost, being 2½*d.* cheaper, but it does not provide enough carbonaceous food, though it does not fall far short of the necessary 23 oz. of nitrogenous substances.

Quantity of Food	Cost		Carbonaceous	Nitrogenous
BREAKFAST—BREAD AND COCOA.	*s.*	*d.*	oz.	oz.
2¼ lb. Bread . . .		3¾	22½	3¾
1½ oz. Cocoa . . .		1½	¾	¼
1 pint Tinned Milk . .		1	1¼	½
2 oz. Sugar . . .		½	1½	—
DINNER—LENTIL SOUP, TOASTED CHEESE.				
1½ lb. Lentils . . .		3	15	6
1 lb. Cheese . . .		8	4½	5½
1½ lb. Bread . . .		2¼	13½	2¼
TEA—RICE PUDDING AND BREAD.				
¾ lb. Rice		1½	10½	¾
1½ pint Tinned Milk .		1½	2¼	1
2 oz. Sugar . . .		¼	1½	—
1½ lb. Bread . . .		2¼	13½	2¼
Total . . .	2	1½	86½	22¼

And how drear and uninteresting is this food compared to that on which people of another class normally live! No refreshing cups of afternoon tea; no pleasant fruit to give interest to the meal. Nothing but dull, keep-me-alive sort of food, and not enough of that to fulfil all Nature's requirements.

But let us take another day's meals, which can consist of hominy, milk, and sugar for breakfast; potato soup and apple-and-sago pudding for dinner; and fish and bread for tea; when fish is plentiful enough to be obtained at 3*d.* a pound, and when apples are to be got at 1½*d.* a pound., which economical housekeepers know is not often the case in London.

Quantity of Food	Cost		Carbonaceous	Nitrogenous
Breakfast—Hominy, Milk, Sugar.	*s.*	*d.*	oz	oz.
1½ lb. Hominy . . .		¾	17¼	3¼
3¼ pints Tinned Milk .		3¼	4½	2¼
6 oz. Sugar . . .		1	4¼	—
Dinner—Potato Soup and Apple-and-Sago Pudding.				
5 lbs. Potatoes . . .		3½	17½	2½
1½ pint Tinned Milk . .		1½	2¼	1
3 oz. Rice		¾	2¼	¼
3 oz. Dripping . . .		1½		—
2½ lb. Apples . . .		3¾	5	1½
6 oz. Sago . . .		¾	3¼	¾
6 oz. Sugar . . .		1	4	—
Tea—Fish and Bread.				
2½ lb. Fish . . .		7½	1¼	7½
2 lb. Bread . . .		3	18	3
1½ pint Tinned Milk . .		1½	2¼	1
3 oz. Sugar . . .		½	2	—
Total . . .	2	5	86	23½

Again, however, we have spent 2*s.* 5*d.* on food, and even now have not got quite sufficient strength-giving or carbonaceous food.

An average of 2*s.* 4*d.* spent daily on food makes a total of 16*s.* 4*d.* at the week's end, leaving the labourer earning his 1*l.* a week 3*s.* 8*d.* with which to pay rent (and decent accommodation of two rooms in London cannot be had for less than 5s. 6d. or 6s. a week); to obtain schooling and lighting; to buy coals, clothes, and boots; to bear the expense of breakages and necessary replacements; to subscribe to a club against sickness or death; and to meet the doctor's bills for the children's illnesses or the wife's confinements. How is it possible? Can 3s. 8d. do so much? No, it cannot; and so food is stinted. The children have to put up with less than they need; the mother 'goes without sooner than let the children suffer,' and thus the new baby is born weakly and but half-nourished; the children develop greediness in their never-satisfied and but partly fed frames; and the father, too often insufficiently sustained, seeks alcohol, which, anyhow, seems to 'pick him up and hold him together,' though his teetotal mates assure him it is only a delusion.

And this is no fancy picture. I have now in my mind one Wilkins, a steady, rough, honest, sober labourer, fairly intelligent, and the father of thirteen children. The two eldest, girls of fourteen and fifteen, are already out at service; but the eleven younger, being under age, are still kept at school and supported by their father. He earns 1l. regularly. They rent the whole house at 12s. a week, and, letting off part, stand themselves at a weekly rent of 5s. for three small rooms. Less than that, as the mother says, 'I could not nohow do with, what with all the washing for such a heavy family, and bathing the little ones, and him coming home tired of an evening, and needing a place to sit down in.' The wife is a decent body, but rough and uncultured; and as she is ignorant of the proper proportions of nitrogenous and carbonaceous substance necessary for the preservation of healthy life, as well as of the kinds of food in which they can be best found, she feeds her family even less nutritiously than she could do if she were better informed. Still the whole wage could only feed them if it were all expended ever so wisely, leaving no margin for the requirements already mentioned.

Take Mrs. Marshall's family and circumstances. Mrs. Marshall is, to all intents and purposes, a widow, her husband being in an asylum. She herself is a superior woman, tall and handsome, and with clean dapper ways and a slight hardness of manner that comes from bitter disappointment and hopeless struggling. She has four children, two of whom have been taken by the Poor Law authorities into their district schools—a better plan than giving out-door relief, but, at the same time, one that has the disadvantage of removing the little ones from the home influence of a very good mother. Mrs. Marshall herself, after vainly trying to get work, was taken as a scrubber at a public institution, where she earns 9s. a week and her dinner. She works from six in the morning till five at night, and then returns to her fireless, cheerless room to find her two children back from school and ready for their chief meal; for during her absence their breakfast and dinner can only have consisted of bread and cold scraps. We will not dwell on the hardship of having to turn to and light the fire, tidy the room, and prepare the meal after having already done ten hours' scrubbing or washing. The financial question is now before us, and to that we will confine our thoughts. Out of her 9s. a week Mrs. Marshall pays 3s. 3d. for rent; 2d. for schooling; 1s. for light and firing (and this does not allow of the children having a morning fire before they go to school); 9*d.* she puts by for boots and clothing; and imagine what it must be to dress, so as to keep warm, three people on 1*l.* 19*s.* a year! and 6*d.* she pays for her bits of washing, for she cannot do them herself after all her heavy daily work. (Pause, though, for a moment to consider how Mrs. Marshall's washerwoman must work when she does three changes of linen, aprons, sheets, and a table-cloth for 6*d.* a week.)

Deduct from the 9*s.* weekly wage—

	s.	*d.*
Rent	3	3
Schooling		2
Firing	1	0
Clothes		9
Washing		6
	5	8

and 3*s.* 4*d.* is left with which to provide breakfast and tea for a hard-working woman for seven days in the week, dinner for Sunday, and three meals daily for two growing children of ten and eleven. We have seen how, even with economy, knowledge, strength, and time, proper food cannot be obtained for less than 1*d.* or 1¼*d.* a meal, and this would make a weekly total of 5*s.* 11¼*d.* 3*s.* 4*d.*, with no time, with little knowledge, and only the remnants of strength, which has been used up in earning the 3*s.* 4*d.*, is all Mrs. Marshall has with which to meet these requirements.

And how do the rich look on these facts? 'Well! nine shillings a week is very fair wage for an unskilled working woman,' was the remark I heard after I had told these facts to mine host at a country house, where we were eating the usual regulation dinner—soup, fish, *entrée*, joint, game, sweets, and hot-house fruits, said with the complacency of satisfaction which follows a glass of good wine. 'Yes, about the cost of your one dinner's wine!' replied one of the guests; but then he was probably one of those ill-balanced people who judge people by what they are rather than by what they have, and he may have thought that the sad, lone woman, with her noble virtues of industry, patience, and self-sacrificing love, had, despite her hard manners, more right to the good things of this world than the suave old man owning fourteen acres of lawn on which no children ever played, and stating, without shame, first, the fact that he used eighty-two tons of coal yearly to warm his own sitting-rooms, and then the opinion that 9*s*. a week was *fair* wage on which to support a good woman and bring up two children.

While this wage is considered a 'fair wage,' the children must remain half-nourished, and grow up incapable of honest toil and valuable effort. While this wage is accepted as a right and normal thing, it is useless to think that the nation will be guided through dangers by means of heavy subscriptions to schools, to hospitals, and sick-asylums. Robust health is impossible; so disease easily finds a home, and teachers vainly try to develop brains ill supplied with blood. By the doorway of semi-starvation disease is invited to enter and find a home among the masses of our wage-earning people.

Before me are the dietary tables of the Whitechapel Workhouse—an institution which stands (thanks to the self-devotion of its able Clerk) high on the list for careful management and economical administration. There are congregated the aged and infirm paupers, and among them are some of Nature's gentlefolk, the old and tired, who, having learnt a few of life's greatest lessons in their long walk through life, ought to be giving them to the young and untried, instead of wearying out their last days in the dull monotony of a useless and regulated existence. Their dietary table allows them for breakfast and supper one pint of tea (made of one ounce to a gallon of water) and five ounces of bread and a tiny bit of butter. For dinner they have meat three times a week, pea-soup and bread twice, suet pudding once, and Irish stew on the other day. For the sake of comparison I will make a food table of this diet, based on the same calculations of food value as those that have been previously made for the family.

Quantity of Food.	Carbonaceous	Nitrogenous.
BREAKFAST AND SUPPER — TEA, BREAD, AND BUTTER.	oz.	oz.
10 oz. Bread	$5\frac{1}{2}$	$\frac{3}{4}$
$\frac{1}{2}$ oz. Butter	$\frac{1}{4}$	—
$\frac{1}{2}$ oz. Sugar	$\frac{1}{2}$	—
$\frac{1}{4}$ pint Milk	less than $\frac{1}{4}$	—
DINNER—MEAT AND POTATOES.		
4 oz. Meat (cooked)	1	1
8 oz. Potatoes	$1\frac{1}{2}$	$\frac{1}{4}$
2 oz. Bread	1	$\frac{1}{4}$
Total	$10\frac{1}{2}$	$2\frac{1}{4}$

Here we see that the total allowance comes only to $10\frac{1}{2}$ oz. of carbonaceous food and $2\frac{1}{4}$ oz. of nitrogenous food, against the estimated quantity of 16 oz. carbonaceous and 4 oz. nitrogenous, which is the necessary allowance for ordinary people, and against the 25 oz. carbonaceous and 5 oz. nitrogenous, which is the regulation diet of the Royal Engineers during peace. It is true that these old folk do not need so much food, for their bodies have ceased to grow and develop, and in aged persons the wear of the frame does not require such replenishment as is the case with young and middle-aged people; but even with this partial diet we find that the cost of maintaining each of these old people is, for food alone, 3s. 11d. per head per week.

Here, then, we have a fact on which a calculation is easy to make, and which, when made, forces us to see that the workman cannot keep his family as well as the pauper is kept. Even on this simple fare it would cost him close on 8s. a week to support himself so as to give him the strength to earn his daily bread; while, if we imagine his family to consist of a wife and six children, we find that his weekly food-bills would amount to 1l. 8s., calculating his requirements on the same basis as in the previous instances.

If we take, therefore, the case of a skilled workman earning his 2l. a week, we still find that, even when adequately fed (and keep in mind the plainness and unattractiveness of the diet), he has only 12s. a week to supply all other necessaries and out of which to lay by, not only against old age and sickness, but against that 'rainy day' and 'out of work from slackness' which so often occur for weeks together in the weather chart of our artisan population.

Or take another case, that of Mr. and Mrs. Stoneman, excellent folk: the wife, a woman of such force and originality of character, such patience and sweet persistency, as would make her an ornament in any class; the husband an honest, steady man, not, perhaps, so clever as his wife, but loving and admiring her none the less for that. They have six children: the two eldest at work; the youngest a sweet tiny thing, as spotlessly clean as water and care can keep it in this mud-coloured atmosphere of Whitechapel. Her husband earns 23s. a week, excepting when bad illness, lasting sometimes six and eight weeks, reduces his wages to nothing; and then the sick man, his wife, and four children have to live, pay rent, firing, and 'doctor's stuff' on the club-money of 14s. a week, for the boys' earnings can only support themselves.

Which of us would consider that he could supply food and sick-luxuries for even *one* person on 14s. a week, the sum fixed by the rich as board wages for an unneeded man-servant?

On the face of it this family is perhaps exceptionally well-off, for the two big lads in it earn, the one 5s. the other 7s. a week, which brings the united weekly wage up to 35s. a week. Mrs. Stoneman is a friend of mine, and, in response to my request, she weighed all the food at every meal, and here is the result.

At the time, however, that this was done Mrs. Stoneman's children had been sent by the Children's Country Holiday Fund into the country for a fortnight's holiday. We must therefore suppose the family to consist only of six, and the necessary quantity of food to sustain them in good healthy working condition would be 76 oz. of carbonaceous food and 19 oz. of nitrogenous food.

SUNDAY MEALS.

Quantity of Food	Cost	Strength-giving.	Flesh-repairing
BREAKFAST—BREAD AND BUTTER AND FISH.	s. d.	oz.	oz.
1¼ lb. Bread	2	11¼	1¾
1½ oz. Butter	1½	1	—
1 Haddock	3	—	—
½ oz. Tea	¾	—	—
2½ oz. Sugar	¼	2	¼
½ pint Tinned Milk . .	½	¾	¼
DINNER—BEEF AND VEGETABLES, APPLE PUDDING.			
1 lb. 3 oz. Beef . . .	1 5	3¼	3¼
3 lb. 10 oz. Potatoes . .	2½	12¼	1¾
1 lb. Beans	2	—	—
3 oz. Bread	¼	1½	—
⅔ lb. Flour	3	8	¾
¼ lb. Lard	2	3	—
1 lb. Apples	2	2	1
1½ oz. Sugar	¼	1	—
TEA—BREAD AND BUTTER.			
¾ lb. Bread	1¼	6¾	2¼
2 oz. Butter	2	1½	—
½ oz. Tea	¼	—	—
2½ oz. Sugar	¼	2	—
½ pint Tinned Milk . .	½	¾	¼
SUPPER—BREAD AND CHEESE.			
1 lb. Bread	1½	9	1½
¼ lb. Cheese	4	1	1¼
Total . .	3 11½	67¾	14¼

WEDNESDAY MEALS

Quantity of Food	Cost	Strength-giving.	Flesh-repairing
BREAKFAST—BREAD AND BUTTER.	s. d.	oz.	oz.
2 lb. Bread	3	18	3
3¼ oz. Butter	3¼	3	—
¼ oz. Tea	¼		—
2 oz. Sugar	¼	1¾	—
½ pint Tinned Milk . .	½	¾	¼

WEDNESDAY MEALS—(*continued*).

Quantity of Food	Cost.	Strength-giving	Flesh-repairing
DINNER—BACON PUDDING.	*s. d.*	oz.	oz.
1 lb. Bacon	6	3	3
2 lb. Potatoes . . .	1¾	7	1
¾ lb. Flour	2	9	¾
2 oz. Suet	1	1½	—
TEA—BREAD AND BUTTER.			
3 lbs. Bread	4½	21	4½
2½ oz. Butter . . .	2½	2	—
½ oz. Tea	1	.	—
2½ oz. Sugar . . .	¾	2	—
½ pint Tinned Milk . .	½	¾	¼
SUPPER—BREAD AND CHEESE.			
¾ lb. Bread	1	6¾	2¼
3 oz. Cheese . .	1½	¾	1
Total	2 6¼	77¼	16

SATURDAY MEALS.

Quantity of Food	Cost	Strength-giving.	Flesh-repairing
BREAKFAST—BREAD AND BUTTER.	*s. d.*	oz.	oz.
1½ lb. Bread	2¼	13½	2¼
3 oz. Butter	3	2¼	—
3½ oz. Sugar	1	3	—
1 pint Tinned Milk .	1½	1¾	¾
DINNER—BREAD AND CHEESE AND COFFEE.			
¾ lb. Bread	1	6¾	2¼
¼ lb. Cheese	4	2¼	2¼
1 pint Milk, Coffee . .	1½	1¾	¾
TEA—BREAD AND BUTTER AND FISH.			
2 lb. 4 oz. Bread . . .	3¼	20½	3¼
2½ oz. Butter	2½	2	—
2 Herrings	2	—	—
2½ oz. Sugar	¾	2	—
½ pint Tinned Milk . .	½	1	½
SUPPER—BREAD AND CHEESE.			
14 oz. Bread	1¼	8½	1
¼ lb. Cheese	2	1	1¼
Total	2 2½	66¾	15¼

This is the food-table of one of the best of managers. It could not well be simpler, and yet we see that it fails every day, sometimes to the extent of one-third, in providing sufficient nitrogenous or flesh-repairing food; but even so the cost for the three days makes a total of 8s. 8½d., or, say, on an average, 3s. a day. Thus it took 1l. 1s. a week to feed this family simply and wholesomely at a time when two of its hungry members of eight and eleven were away. The weekly rent to house it in two rooms takes 5s. 7d.; to educate the school-going members, 7d. a week must be paid; to keep the fire and lights going (and this, of course, is more expensive than if the fuel could be got in in large quantities) demands 2s. 6d. a week; and to provide washing materials another 1s. must be deducted.

When these outgoings are met there remains but 4s. 1d. with which to provide the food of the two then absent children, to pay club subscriptions for three people (because each of the working members is in a sick-club and burial club), to procure boots, clothes, and to lay by against the days of illness, slackness, and old age.

Now these are the facts which, summed up in a sentence, amount to this, that while wages are at the present rate the large mass of our people cannot get enough food to maintain them in robust health, and bodily health is here alone considered.

No mention has been made of the food a man requires to keep his whole nature in robust health; of the books, the means of culture, the opportunities of social intercourse, which are as necessary for his mental health and development as food and drink are for his bodily. No account has been taken of all that each human being needs to keep his spiritual nature alive. The quiet times in the country or by the sea, the knowledge of Nature's mysteries, the opportunities for the cultivation of natural affection. 'Yes, it is seven years since me and my daughter met,' I heard a gentle old lady of sixty-nine say the other day, one of God's aristocracy, the upper class in virtue and unselfishness. 'You see, she lives a pretty step from here, and moving about is not to be thought of when money is so scarce.'

The body's needs are the most exacting; they make themselves felt with daily recurring persistency, and, while they remain unsatisfied, it is hard to give time or thought to the mental needs or the spiritual requirements; but if our nation is to be wise and righteous, as well as healthy and strong, they must be considered. A fair wage must allow a man, not only to adequately feed himself and his family, but also to provide the means of mental cultivation and spiritual development. Indeed, some humanitarians assert that it should be sufficient to give him a home wherein he may rest from noise, with books, pictures, and society; and there are those who go so far as to suggest that it should be sufficient to enable him to learn the larger lessons which travellers gain from other nations, as well as the teaching which the great dumb teachers wait to impart to 'those with ears to hear' of fraternity, purity, and eternal hope.

Why is it that our wage-earners cannot get this? Why is it that, as we indulge in such dreams, they sound impossible and almost impracticable, though no reader of this Review will add undesirable? Is it because our nation has not fought Ignorance, with pointed weapons, and by its knights of proved prowess and valour? Or is it because our rulers have not recognised the Greed of certain classes or individuals as a national evil, and struggled against it with the strength of unity? It cannot be the want of money in our land which causes so many to be half-fed and cry silently from want of strength to make a noise. As we stand at Hyde Park Corner, or wander in among the miles of streets of 'gentlemen's residences' in the West End, our hearts are gladdened at the sight of the wealth that is in our land; but they would be glad with a deeper gladness if Wilkins was not getting slowly brutalised by his struggle, if there were a chance of Alice and Johnnie Marshall growing up as Nature meant them to grow, or if clever Mrs. Stoneman's patient efforts could be crowned with success. Money in plenty is in our midst, but cruel, blinding Poverty keeps her company, and our nation cannot boast herself of her wealth while half her people are but partly fed, and too poor to use their minds or to aspire after holiness.

By the optimist we may be told that all mention of charitable aid has been omitted; that in such a case as that of Wilkins, or of Mrs. Marshall, there would be aid from the philanthropic; that old clothes would do something to replenish the wardrobe, otherwise to be kept supplied by 1*l*. 19*s*. a year; and that scraps and broken victuals find their way from most back-doors into the homes of the poor. But, though this may be true when the poor are scattered among the rich, it is not true of that neighbourhood which I know best, where through miles of streets the income of each resident does not exceed thirty shillings a week, and where the four-roomed houses (as a rule, let out to two or three families) are unrelieved by a single house inhabited by only one family, or where they 'keeps a servant.'

The advocates of children's penny dinners may take these facts as a strong argument in favour of their scheme, and feel that in this simple method is the solution of the difficulty. But those who so think cannot have considered the question in all its bearings. If feeding the children enables us to limit the power of disease, it does so by putting fresh weapons into the hands of the Greed of certain classes or individuals, which is so ill-curbed and ineffectively conquered as to be nothing loth to take advantage of every opportunity of working its cruel will.

If the children are fed at school it enables the mother to go out to work. The supply of female labour is thus increased, and married women can offer their work at lower wages than widows or single ones, because their labour is only supplementary to that of their husbands. The consequence is that wages go down, because more women are in the labour market than are needed, and those get the work who will take it for the least remuneration. Thus, though Mrs. Harris may get work, her children being 'now fed by the ladies round at the school,' she does so at the expense of lowering Jane Metcalf's wages; and, as Jane is working to help her widowed mother to keep the four younger children off the parish, the only result is that Tommie and Lizzie and the two baby Metcalfs get worse food, and Jane finds life harder, and sometimes sees temptation through magnifying-glasses.

Besides these economic results which must inevitably follow the plan of feeding the children on any large scale, there are others which ensue from the lightening of parental responsibility, and these everyone who knows the poor can foresee without the gift of prophecy; the idle father is made more idle, the gossiping mother less controlled, and from the drunken parent is taken the last feeble bond which binds him to sobriety and its hopeful consequences. But perhaps as important as any of these results is the evil which follows the taking the children from the home influence. In our English love of home is one of our hopes for the future; and not the least conspicuous as a moral training-ground is the family dinner-table. There the mother can teach the little lessons of good manners and neat ways, and the larger truths of unselfishness and thoughtfulness. There the whole family can meet, and from the talks over meals, during the time which, as things now are, is perhaps the only leisure of the busy mechanic, may grow that sympathy between the older and younger people which must refresh and gladden both. No; it is not by any charitable effort that this poverty must be fought. A national want must be met by a national effort, and the thought of the political economist, which has hitherto been devoted to the question of production and accumulation of wealth, must now turn its attention to the problem of its right use and distribution, recognising that 'the wise use of wealth in developing a complete human life is of incomparably the greater moment both to men and nations.' While more than half the English people are unable to live their best life or reach their true standard of humanity, it is useless to congratulate ourselves on our national supremacy or class our nation as wealthy.

Some economists will reply that these sad conditions

are but the result of our freedom; that the boasted 'liberty' in our land must result in the few strong making themselves stronger, and in the many weak suffering from their weakness. But is this necessarily so? Is this the only result to be expected from human beings having the power to act as they please? Are not love, goodwill, and social instincts as truly parts of human character as greed, selfishness, and sulkiness; and may we not believe that human nature is great enough to care to use its freedom for the good of all? Men have done noble things to obtain this freedom. They have loved her with the ardour of a lover's love, with the patience of a silver wedded life; and now that they have her, is she only to be used to injure the weak, and to make life cruel and almost impossible to the large majority? 'What is the right use of freedom?' The ancient answer was, 'To love God.' And can we love God whom we have not seen when we love not our brother whom we have seen?

HENRIETTA O. BARNETT.

II.

RELIEF FUNDS AND THE POOR.[1]

The poverty of the poor and the failure of the Mansion House Relief Fund are the facts which stand out from the gloom of a winter when dark weather, dull times, and discontent united to depress both the hopes of the poor and the energy of their friends. The memory of days full of unavailing complaint and of aimless pity is one from which all minds readily turn, quieting their fears with the assumption that the poverty was exaggerated or that the generosity of the rich is ample for all occasions.

The facts, however, remain that the poor are very poor, and that the fund failed as a means of relief; and these facts must be faced if a lesson is to be learnt from the past, and a way discovered through the perils of the future. The policies which occupy the leaders' minds, the interests of business, the theologies, the fashions, are but webs woven in the trees while the storm is rising in the distance. Sounds of the storm are already in the air, a murmuring among those who have not enough, puffs of boasting from those who have too much, and a mutter-

[1] Reprinted, by permission, from the *Nineteenth Century* of November 1886.

ing from those who are angry because while some are drunken others are starving. The social question is rising for solution, and, though for a moment it is forgotten, it will sweep to the front and put aside as cobwebs the ' deep ' concerns of leaders and teachers. The danger is lest it be settled by passion and not by reason, lest, that is, reforms be hurriedly undertaken in answer to some cry, and without consideration of facts, their weight, their causes, and their relation.

The study of the condition of the people receives hardly as much attention as that which Sir J. Lubbock gives to the ants and the wasps. Bold good men discuss the poor, and cheques are given by irresponsible benefactors; but there are few students who reverently and patiently make observations on social conditions, accumulate facts, and watch cause and effect. Scientific method has won the great victories of the day, and scientific method is supreme everywhere except in those human affairs which most concern humanity.

Ten years ago Arnold Toynbee demanded a ' body of doctrine ' from those who cared for the poor. He sought an intellectual basis for moral fervour, and yet to-day what a muck-heap is our social legislation, what a confusion of opinion there exists about the poor law, education, emigration, and land laws! All reformers are driving on; but what is each driving at? Sometimes the same driver has aims obviously incompatible, as when the Lord Mayor one day signs a report which says that ' the spasmodic assistance given by the public in answer to special appeals is really useless,' and another day himself inaugurates a relief fund by a special appeal.

One of the facts made evident last winter is the poverty

of the poor, and it is a fact about which the public mind is uncertain.

The working men when they appear at meetings seem to be well dressed in black cloth, the statistics of trades-unions, friendly, co-operative, and building societies show the members to be so numerous, and the accumulated funds to be so far above thousands and so near to millions sterling, that the necessary conclusion is, 'There is no poverty among the poor.' But then the clergy or missionaries echo some 'bitter cry,' and tell how there are thousands of working folk in danger of starvation, thousands without warmth or clothing, and the necessary conclusion is, 'All the poor are poverty-stricken.' The public mind halts between these two conclusions and is uncertain.

The uncertainty is due partly to the vague use of the term 'poor,' by which is generally meant all those who are not tradespeople or capitalists, and partly to an inability to appreciate the size of London. The poor, it is obvious, form only a minority in the community, and a minority suggests something unimportant, and notwithstanding the size of London, it is regarded as a small and manageable body.

Last winter's experience clears away all uncertainty, and shows that there is a vast mass of people in London who have neither black coats nor savings, and whose life is dwarfed and shortened by want of food and clothing. In Whitechapel there is a population of 70,000: of these some 20 per cent., exclusive of the Jewish population, applied at the office of the Mansion House Relief Fund during the three months it was opened. In St. George's, East, there is a population of 50,000, and of these 29 per cent. applied. Among all who applied the number belonging to any trades-union or friendly society was very few. In Whitechapel only six out of 1,700 applicants were members of a benefit club. In St. George's only 177 out of 3,578 called themselves artisans. In Stepney 1,000 men applied before one mechanic came, and only one member of a trades-union came under notice at all. In the Tower Hamlets division of East London out of a population of 500,000, 17,384 applied, representing 86,920 persons. It may be safely assumed that all in need did not apply, and that many thousands were assisted by other agencies. The reports of some of the visitors expressly state that the numbers they give are exclusive of many referred to the Jewish Board of Guardians, the clergy, and other agencies, while numbers of those who did apply either did not wait to have their names entered or were so manifestly beyond the reach of money help that they were not recorded among applicants. Especially noteworthy among the remarks of the visitors is one, that all who applied would at any season of the year apply in the same way and give the same evidence of poverty. 'If a fund was advertised as largely as this fund has been in summer, and when trade was at its best, precisely the same people would apply.' The truth of the remark has been put to the test, and during the summer a large number of those relieved in the winter have been visited, with the result that they have been found apparently in like misery and equally in need of assistance.

Of the poverty of those who made application there has been no question. Some may have brought it on themselves by drink or by vice, some may have been thriftless and without self-control; but all were poor, so poor as to be without the things necessary for mere existence. The men and women who crowded the relief offices had haggard and drawn faces, their worn and thin bodies shivered under their rags of clothing, and they gave no sign of strength or of hope. Their homes were squalid, the children ill-fed, ill-clad, and joyless, their record showed that for months they had received no regular wage, and that their substance was more often at the pawnbroker's than in the home.

Last winter's experience shows that outside the classes of regular wage-earning workmen, who are often included among 'the poor,' is a mass of people numbering some tens of thousands who are without the means of living. These are the poor, and their poverty is the common concern.

Statistics prove what has long been known to those whose business lies in poor places, and to them the reports of the increased prosperity of the country have been like songs of gladness in a land of sorrow. They know the streets in which every room is a home, the homes in which there is no comfort for the sick, no easy-chair for the weary, no bath for the tired, no fresh air, no means of keeping food, no space for play, no possibility of quiet, and to them the news of the national wealth and the sight of fashionable luxury seem but cruel satire. The little dark rooms may bear traces of the man's struggle or of the woman's patience, but the homes of the poor are sad, like the fields of lost battles, where heroism has fought in vain. By no struggle and by no patience can health be won in so few feet of cubic air, and no parent dares to hope that he can make the time of youth so joyful as to for ever hold his children to pleasures which are pure. The homes of the poor are a mockery of the name, but yet how many would think themselves happy if even such homes were secure, and if they were able to look to the future without seeing starvation for their children and the workhouse for themselves! One example will illustrate many. The Browns are a family of five; they occupy one room. The man is a labourer, London-born, quick-witted and slow-bodied, and, as many labourers do, he fills up slack time with hawking; the woman takes in her neighbours' washing. Their room, twelve feet by ten feet, is crowded with two bedsteads, the implements for washing, the coal-bin, a table, a chest, and a few chairs; on the walls are some pictures, the human protest against the doctrine that the poor can 'live by bread alone.' The man earns sometimes 3s., often nothing, in the day; and his wife brings in sometimes 6d. or 9d. a day, but her work fills the room with damp and discomfort, and almost necessarily keeps the husband out of doors. Both man and woman are still young, but they look aged, and the children are thin and delicate. They seldom have enough to eat and never enough to wear, they are rarely healthy, and are never so happy as to thank God for their creation. Hard work will make these children orphans, or bad air, cold, and hunger will make these parents childless.

In the case of another family, where the wage is regular—the income is 1*l.* a week—the outlook is not much brighter. Here there is the same crowded room, for which 3s. a week is paid, the same weary, half-starved faces, the same want of air and water. Here, too, the parents dare not look forwards, because even if the income remains permanent, it cannot secure necessaries for sickness, it cannot educate or apprentice the children, and it cannot provide for their own old age. No income, however, does remain permanent, and the regular hand is always anxious lest a change in trade, or in his employer's temper, may send him adrift.

In the cases where there is drink, carelessness, or idleness everything of course looks worse. The room is poorer and dirtier, the faces more shrunken, and the clothes thinner. Indignation against sin does not settle the matter. The poverty is manifest, and if the cause be in the weakness of human nature, then the greater and the harder is the duty of effecting its cure.

Cases of poverty such as these are common; they who by business, duty, or affection go among the poor know of their existence; but if those who hire a servant, employ workpeople, or buy cheap articles would think about what they talk, they could not longer content themselves with phrases about thrift as almighty for good, and intemperance as almighty for evil. Fourteen pounds a year, if a domestic servant has unfailing health and unbroken work from the age of twenty to fifty-five, will only enable her to save enough for her old age by giving up all pleasure, by neglecting her own family duties, and by impoverishing her life to make a livelihood. Very sad is it to meet in some back-room the living remains of an old servant. Mrs. Smith is sixty-five years old; she has been all her life in service, and saved over 100*l*. She has had but little joy in her youth, and now in her old age she is lonely. Her fear is lest, spending only 7*s*. a week, her savings may not last her life. She could hardly have done more, and what she did was not enough.

A wage of 20s. or 25s. a week is called good wages, yet it leaves the earners unable to buy sufficient food or to procure any means of recreation. The following table[1] represents the necessary weekly expenditure of a family of eight persons, of whom six are children. It allows for each day no cheering luxuries, but only the bare amount of carbonaceous and nitrogenous foods which are absolutely necessary for the maintenance of the body.

	£	s.	d.
Food, i.e. oatmeal, 1½lb. of meat a day among eight persons, cocoa and bread	0	11	0
Rent for two small rooms	0	5	0
Schooling for four children	0	0	4
Washing	0	1	0
Firing and light	0	2	6
Total	1	2	10

If to this 2s. a week be added for clothes (and what woman dressing on 100l. or 80l. a year could allow less than 5l. a year to clothe a working man, his wife, and six children) then the necessary weekly expenditure of the family is 1l. 4s. 10d. Few fathers or mothers are able to resist, or ought to resist, the temptation of taking or giving some pleasure; so even where work is regular, and paid at 1l. 5s. a week, there must be in the home want of food as well as of the luxuries which gladden life.

Those dwellers in pleasant places, without experience of the homes of the poor, who will resolutely set themselves to think about what they do know must realise that those who make cheap goods are too poor to

---

[1] This table is taken from a paper written by my wife in the *National Review*, July 1886, in which she illustrates by many examples that the average wage is insufficient to support life.

do their duty to themselves, their neighbours, and their country. The mystery, indeed, remains, how many manage to live at all.

One solution is that there exists among these irregular workers a kind of communism. They prefer to occupy the same neighbourhood and make long journeys to work rather than go to live among strangers. They easily borrow and easily lend. The women spend much time in gossiping, know intimately one another's affairs, and in times of trouble help willingly. One couple, whose united earnings have never reached 15s. a week, whose home has never been more than one small room, has brought up in succession three orphans. The old man, at seventy years of age, just earns a living by running messages or by selling wirework: but even now he spends many a night in hushing a baby whose desertion he pities, and whom he has taken to his care.

The poverty of the poor is understood by the poor, and their charity is according to the measure of Christ's. The charity of the rich is according to another measure, because they do not know of poverty, and they do not know because they no not think. Only the self-satisfied Pharisee and the proud Roman could pass Calvary unmoved, and only the self-absorbed can be ignorant that every day the innocent and helpless are crucified. The selfishness of modern life is shown most clearly in this absence of thought. Absorbed in their own concerns, kindly people carelessly hear statements, see prices, and face sights which imply the ruin of their fellow-creatures. The rich would not be so cruel if they would think. Thought about the amount of food which 'good wages' can buy, about the hours spent in making matches or coats, about the sorrows behind the faces of those who serve them in shops or pass them in the streets; thought would make the rich ready to help; and the fact that there are among the 500,000 inhabitants of the Tower Hamlets 86,920 too poor to live is enough to make them think.

The failure of the relief fund is the other fact of the winter to stir thought.

Mansion House relief represents the mercies to which the wisdom and the love of the completest age have committed the needs of the poor. Never were needs so delicate left to mercies so clumsy; needs intertwined with the sorrows and sufferings with which no stranger could intermeddle have been met with the brutal generosity of gifts given often with little thought or cost. The result has been an increase of the causes which make poverty and a decrease of good-will among men.

The fund failed even to relieve distress. In St. George's-in-the-East there were nearly 4,000 applicants, representing 20,000 persons. All of these were in distress—were, that is, cold and hungry. Of these there were 2,400 applicants, representing some 12,000 persons—whom the committee considered to be working people unemployed and within the scope of the fund. For their relief 2,000*l*. was apportioned; and if it had been equally divided each person would have had 3*s*. 4*d*. on which to support life during three months. Such sums might have relieved the givers, pleased by the momentary satisfaction of the recipient, but they would not have relieved the poor, who would still have had to endure days and weeks of want.

The fund was thus in the first place inadequate to relieve the distress. An attempt was made in some districts by discrimination to make it useful to those who were 'deserving.' Forms were given out to be filled in by applicants; visitors were appointed to visit the homes and to make inquiries; committees sat daily to consider and decide on applications. The end of all has been that in one district those assisted were found to be 'improvident, unsober, and non-industrious,' and in another the almoner can only say, 'they are a careless, hard-living, hard-drinking set of people, and are so much what their circumstances have made them that terms of moral praise or blame are hardly applicable.'

An analysis of the decisions of the committees formed in the various parts of the Tower Hamlets shows that the decisions were according to different standards, and with different views of what was meant by 'assistance.' A half-crown a week was voted for the support of one family in which the man was a notorious drunkard. Twelve pounds were given to start a costermonger on one day, while at a subsequent committee meeting 10s. was voted for a family in almost identical circumstances. In one district casual labourers were given 20s. or 30s., but in the neighbouring district casual labourers were refused relief.

Methods of relief were as many as were the districts into which London was divided. In Whitechapel a labour test was applied. The labourers were offered street-sweeping; and those who were used only to indoor work were put to whitewashing, window-cleaning, or tailoring. The women were given needlework. When it was known to the large crowd brought to the office by the advertisement of the fund that work was to be offered to the able-bodied, there was among the ne'er-do-weels great indignation. 'Call this charity!' 'We will complain to the Lord Mayor, we will break windows,' and addressing the almoners, 'It is you fellows who are getting 1*l*. a day for your work.' Many 'finding they could not get relief without doing work did not persist in their application,' and they were not entered as applicants, but work was actually offered to 850 men and accepted by only 339. Of these the foreman writes, 'The labour test was a sore trial for a great many of them. I repeatedly had it said to me by them, "The Fund is a charity, and we ought not to work for it."'

In St. George's there was no labour test, and there 1,689 men and 682 women received assistance in food or in materials for labour. In Stepney the conditions under which the Fund was collected were strictly observed, and only those 'out of employment through the present depression' were assisted. The consequence was that casual labourers, the sick, the aged, all known to be frequently out of work, were refused, and much of the Fund was spent in large sums for the emigration of a few. In this district the committee was largely composed of members of friendly societies, men who, by experience, were familiar both with the habits of the poor and with the methods of relief. Their co-operation was invaluable, both in itself and also for the confidence which it won for the administration.

In Mile End the committee had another standard of character and another method of inquiry. No record was kept of the number of applications, and those relieved have been differently described as 'good men' and 'loafers' by different members of the committee.

D

2,539*l*. were spent among 2,133 families, an average of 4s. 10*d*. a person. The Poplar Committee has published no report, but one of its members writes : 'Relief was often given without investigation to old, chronic, sick, and poor-law cases, without distinction as to character ; the rule was, Give, give! spend, spend!' and another states the opinion 'that the whole neighbourhood was demoralised by the distribution of the Fund.' As a result of their experiences, some of those engaged in relief in this district are now making efforts to unite workmen, and the members of benefit societies, in the administration of future funds.

The sort of relief given was as various as the methods of relief. Sometimes money, sometimes tickets, sometimes food; the variety is excused by one visitor, who says, 'We were ten days at work before instructions came from the Mansion House, and then it was too late to change our system.' Discrimination utterly broke down, and with all the appliances it was chance which ruled the decision. The gifts fell on the worthy and on the unworthy, but as they fell only in partial showers, none received enough and many who were worthy went empty away.

Discrimination of desert is indeed impossible. The poor-law officials, with ample time and long experience, cannot say who deserves or would be benefited by out-relief. Amateurs appointed in a hurry, and confused by numbers, vainly try to settle desert. Systems must adopt rules; friendship alone can settle merit.

The Fund failed to relieve distress, and further developed some of the causes which make poverty.

Prominent among such causes are (1) faith in chance ;

(2) dishonesty in its fullest sense; (3) the unwisdom of so-called charity.

(1) The big advertisement of '70,000*l*. to be given away' offered a chance which attracted idlers, and relaxed in many the energies hitherto so patiently braced to win a living for wife or children. The effect is frequently noticed in the reports. The St. George's-in-the-East visitors emphasise the opinion that it was 'the great publicity of the Fund which made its distribution so difficult.' A visitor in Poplar thinks 'the publicity was tempting to bad cases and deterrent of good ones.' The chance of a gift out of so big a sum was too good to be missed for the sake of hard work and small wages.

Faith in chance was further encouraged by the irregular methods of administration. Refusals and relief followed no law discoverable by the poor. In the same street one washerwoman was set up with stock, while another in equal circumstances was dismissed. In adjoining districts such various systems were adopted that of three 'mates' one would receive work, another a gift, and the third nothing. 'The power of chance' was the teaching of the Fund, started through the accidental emotions of a Lord Mayor, and they who believe in chance give up effort, become wayward, and lose power of mind and body. Chance leads her followers to poverty, and the increase of the spirit of gambling is not the least among the causes of distress.

(2) The remark is sometimes made that 'the righteous man is never found begging his bread,' or, in other words, that there is always work for the man who can be trusted. Honesty in its fullest sense, implying

absolute truth, thoroughness, and responsibility, has great value in the labour market, and agencies which increase a trust in honesty increase wealth. The tendency of the Fund has been to create a trust in lies. Its organisation of visitors and committees offered a show of resistance to lies, but over such resistance lies easily triumphed, and many notorious evil-livers got by a good story the relief denied to others. Anecdotes are common as to the way in which visitors were deceived, committees hoodwinked, and money wrongly gained, while the better sort of poor, failing to understand how so much money could have had so little effect, hold the officials to have been smart fellows who took care of themselves. The laughter roused by such talk is the laughter which demoralises, it is the praise of the power of lies, and the laughers will not be among those who by honesty do well for themselves and for others.

(3) The mischief of foolish charity is a text on which much has been written, but no doubt exists as to the power of wise charity. The teaching which fits the young to do better work or to find resource in a bye-trade, the influence by which the weak are strengthened to resist temptation, the application of principles which will give confidence, and the setting up of ideals which will enlarge the limits of life—this is the charity which conquers poverty. In East London there are many engaged in such charity, and to their work the action of the Fund was most prejudicial. Some of them, carried away by the excitement, relaxed their patient, silent efforts, while they tried to meet a thousand needs with no other remedy than a gift. Others saw their work spoiled, their lessons of self-help undone by the offer of

a dole, their teaching of the duty of helping others forgotten in the greedy scramble for graceless gifts. They devoted themselves to do their utmost and bore the heavy burden of distributing the Fund, but most of them speak sadly of their experience. They laboured sometimes for sixteen hours a day, but their labour was not to do good but to prevent evil—a labour of pain—and one, speaking the experience of his fellows, says 'their labours had the appearance of a hurried and spasmodic effort.' The fund of charity, like a torrent, swept away the tender plants which the stream of charity had nourished.

In the face of all this experience it is not extravagant to say that the means of relief used last winter developed the causes of poverty. It may be that if all the poor were self-controlled and honest, and if all charity were wise, poverty would still exist; but self-indulgence, lies, and unwise charity are causes of poverty, and these causes have been strengthened. One visitor's report sums up the whole matter when it says:—

They (the applicants) have received their relief, and they are now in much the same position as they were before, and as they will be found, it is feared, in future winters, until more effectual and less spasmodic means of improving their condition can be devised, for the causes of distress are chronic and permanent. The foundation of such independence of character as they possessed has been shaken, and some of them have taken the first step in mendicancy, which is too often never retraced.

Examples, of course, may be found where the relief has been helpful, and some visitors, in the comtemplation of the worthy family relieved from pressure and set free to work, may think that one such result justifies many failures. It is not, though, expedient that many should suffer for one, or that a population should be demoralised in order that two or three might have enough.

The Fund as a means of relief has failed: it is condemned by the recipients, who are bitter on account of disappointed hopes; by the almoners, whose only satisfaction is that they managed to do the least possible mischief; and by the mechanics, whose name was taken in vain by the agitators who went to the Lord Mayor, and who feel their class degraded by a system of relief which assumes improvidence and imposition among working men.

The failure of the latest method of relief has been made as manifest as the poverty, and no prophet is needed to tell that bad times are coming. The outlook is most gloomy. The August reports of trades societies characterise trade as 'dull' or 'very slack.' The pawnbrokers report in the same month that they are taking in rather than handing out pledges, and all those who have experience of the poor consider poverty to be chronic. If not in the coming winter, still in the near future there must be trouble.

Poverty in London is increasing both relatively and actually. Relative poverty may be lightly considered, but it breeds trouble as rapidly as actual poverty. The family which has an income sufficient to support life on oatmeal will not grow in good-will when they know that daily meat and holidays are spoken of as 'necessaries' for other workers and children. Education and the spread of literature have raised the standard of living, and they who cannot provide boots for their children, nor sufficient fresh air, nor clean clothes, nor means of pleasure, feel themselves to be poor, and have the hopelessness which is the curse of poverty, as selfishness is the curse of wealth.

Poverty, however, in East London, is increasing actually. It is increased (1) by the number of incapables: 'broken men, who by their misfortunes or their vices have fallen out of regular work,' and who are drawn to East London because chance work is more plentiful, 'company' more possible, and life more enlivened by excitement. (2) By the deterioration of the physique of those born in close rooms, brought up in narrow streets, and early made familiar with vice. It was noticed that among the crowds who applied for relief there were few who seemed healthy or were strongly grown. In Whitechapel the foreman of those employed in the streets reported that 'the majority had not the stamina to make even a good scavenger.' (3) By the disrepute into which saving is fallen. Partly because happiness (as the majority count happiness) seems to be beyond their reach, partly because the teaching of the example of the well-to-do is 'enjoy yourselves,' and partly because 'the saving man' seems 'bad company, unsocial and selfish'; the fact remains that few take the trouble to save—only units out of the thousands of applicants had shown any signs of thrift. (4) By the growing animosity of the poor against the rich. Good-will among men is a source of prosperity as well as of peace. Those bound together consider one another's interests, and put the good of the 'whole' before the good of a class. Among large classes of the poor animosity is slowly taking the place of good-will, the rich are held to be of another nation, the theft of a lady's diamonds is not always condemned as the theft of a poor man's money, and the gift of 70,000*l*. is looked on as ransom and perhaps an inadequate ransom. The bitter remarks sometimes heard by the almoners are signs of disunion, which will decrease the resources of all classes. The fault did not begin with the poor; the rich sin, but the poor, made poorer and more angry, suffer the most.

On account of these and other causes it may be expected that poverty will be increased. The poorer quarters will become still poorer, the sight of squalor, misery, and hunger more painful, the cry of the poor more bitter. For their relief no adequate means are proposed. The last twenty years have been years of progress, but for lack of care and thought the means of relief for poverty remain unchanged. The only resource twenty years ago was a Mansion House Fund, and the only resource available in this enlightened and wealthy year of our Lord is a similar gift thrown—not brought—from the West to the East.

The paradise in which a few theorists lived, listening to the talk at social science congresses, has been rudely broken. Lord Mayors, merchant princes, prime ministers, and able editors have no better means for relief of distress than that long ago discredited by failure. One of the greatest dangers possible to the State has been growing in the midst, and the leaders have slumbered and slept. The resources of civilisation, which are said to be ample to suppress disorder and to evolve new policies, have not provided means by which the chief commandment may be obeyed, and love shown to the poor neighbour.

The outlook is gloomy enough, and the cure of the evil is not to be effected by a simple prescription. The cure must be worked by slow means which will take account of the whole nature of man, which will consider the future to be as important as the present, and which will win by waiting.

Generally it is assumed that the chief change is that to be effected in the habits of the poor. All sorts of missions and schemes exist for the working of this change. Perhaps it is more to the purpose that a change should be effected in the habits of the rich. Society has settled itself on a system which it never questions, and it is assumed to be absolutely within a man's right to live where he chooses and to get the most for his money.

It is this practice of living in pleasant places which impoverishes the poor. It authorises, as it were, a lower standard of life for the neighbourhoods in which the poor are left; it encourages a contempt for a home which is narrow; it leaves large quarters of the town without the light which comes from knowledge, and large masses of the people without the friendship of those better taught than themselves. The precept that 'every one should live over his shop' has a very direct bearing on life, and it is the absence of so many from their shops, be the shop 'the land' or 'a factory,' which makes so many others poorer.

Absenteeism is an acknowledged cause of Irish troubles, and Mr. Goldwin Smith has pointed out that 'the greatest evils of absenteeism are — first, that it withdraws from the community the upper class, who are the natural channels of civilising influences to the classes below them; and, secondly, that it cuts off all personal relations between the individual landlord and his tenant.' He further adds that it was 'natural the gentry should avoid the sight of so much wretchedness ... and be drawn to the pleasures of London or Dublin.' The result in Ireland was heartbreaking poverty which relief funds did not relieve, and there is no reason why in East London absenteeism should have other results.

In the same way the unquestioned habit by which every one thinks himself justified in getting the most for his money tends to make poverty. In the competition which the habit provokes many are trampled underfoot, and in the search after enjoyment wealth is wasted which would support thousands in comfort.

The habits of the people are in the charge of the Church, so that by its ministers (conformist and non-conformist) God's Spirit may bend the most stubborn will. Those ministers have a great responsibility. God's Spirit has been imprisoned in phrases about the duty of contentment and the sin of drink; the stubborn will has been strengthened by the doctor's opinion as to the necessity of living apart from the worry of work, and by the teaching of a political economy which assumes that a man's might is a man's right. The ministers who would change the habits of the rich will have to preach the prophet's message about the duty of giving and the sin of luxury, and to denounce ways of business now pronounced to be respectable and Christian. Old teaching will have to be put in new language, giving shown to consist in sharing, and earning to be sacrifice. For some time it may be the glory of a preacher to empty rather than to fill his church as he reasons about the Judgment to come, when 'twopence a gross to the matchmakers will be laid alongside of the twenty-two per cent. to the shareholders,' and penny dinners for the poor compared with the sixteen courses for the rich—when the 'seamy' side of wealth and pleasures will be exposed.[1] For some time the ministers who would change habits may fail to attract congregations. It is not until they are able again to lift up the God whose presence is dimly felt, and whose nature is misunderstood, that they will succeed. In the knowledge of God is eternal life. When all know God as the Father who requires rich and poor to be perfect sharers in His gifts of virtue, forgiveness, and peace, then none will be satisfied until they are at one with Him, and His habit has become their habit.

It may, however, be well here to suggest in a few words what may be done while habits remain the same by laws or systems for the relief of poverty.

It would be wise (1) to promote the organisation of unskilled labour. The mass of applicants last winter belonged to this class, and in one report it is distinctly said that the greater number were 'born within the demoralising influence of the intermittent and irregular employment given by the Dock Companies, and who have never been able to rise above their circumstances.' It is in evidence that the wages of these men do not exceed 12s. a week on an average in a year. If, by some encouragement, these men could be induced to form a union, and if by some pressure the Docks could be induced to employ a regular gang, much would be gained.

---

[1] Prices paid according to the Mansion House report are: Making of shirts, $\frac{3}{4}d.$ each; making soldiers' leggings, 2s. a dozen; making lawn-tennis aprons, elaborately frilled, $5\frac{1}{2}d.$ a dozen to the sweater, the actual worker getting less.

The very organisation would be a lesson to these men in self-restraint and in fellowship. The substitution of regular hands at the Docks for those who now, by waiting and scrambling, get a daily ticket would give to a large number of men the help of settled employment and take away the dependence on chance, which makes many careless. Such a change might be met by a *non possumus* of the directors, but it is forgotten that to the present system a weightier *non possumus* would be urged if the labourers could speak as shareholders now speak. A possible loss of profit is not comparable to an actual loss of life, and the labourers do lose life and more than life as they scramble for a living that the dividend or salaries may be increased.

(2) The helpers of the poor might be efficiently organised. The ideal of co-operating charity has long hovered over the mischief and waste of competing charity. Up to the present, denominational jealousy, or the belief in crochets, or the self-will which 'dislikes committees' has prevented common work. If all who are serving the poor could meet and divide—meet to learn one another's object and divide each to do his own work—there would be a force applied which might remove mountains of difficulty. Abuse would be known, wise remedies would be suggested, and foolish remedies prevented. Indirect means would be brought to the support of direct, and those concerned to reform the land laws, to teach the ignorant, and beautify the ugly would be recognised as fellow-workers with those whose object is the abolition of poverty. Money would be amply given, and the high motives of faith and love applied to the reform of character. The ideal is in its fulness impos-

sible until there be a really national Church, in which the denominations will each preach their truth, and in which 'the entire religious life of the nation will be expressed.' Such a Church, extending into every corner of the land and drawing to itself all who love their neighbours, would realise the ideal of co-operative charity, and so order things that no one would be in sorrow whom comfort will relieve, and no one in pain whom help can succour.

(3) Lastly, the qualification for a seat on a board of guardians might be removed and the position opened to working men.[1] The action of the poor-law has a very distinct effect on poverty, and intelligent experience is on the side of administration by rule rather than by sentiment. In poor-law unions, where it is known that 'indoors' all that is necessary for life will be provided, but that 'outdoors' nothing will be given, the poor feel they are under a rule which they can understand. They are able to calculate on what will happen in a way which is impossible when 'giving goes by favour or desert,' and they do not wait and suffer by trusting to a chance. Public opinion, however, does not support such administration, and as public opinion is largely now that of the working men, it is necessary that these men should be admitted on to boards of guardians, where by experience they would learn how impossible it is to adjust relief to desert, and how much less cruel is regular sternness than spasmodic kindness. A carefully and wisely adminis-

---

[1] It might be necessary at the same time to abolish 'the compounder,' so that the tenant of every tenement might himself pay the rates and feel their burden.

tered poor-law is the best weapon in hand for the troubles to come, and such is impossible without the sympathy of all classes.

By some such means preparation may be made for dealing with poverty, but even these would not be sufficient and would not be in order at a moment of emergency.

If next winter there be great distress, what, it may be asked, can possibly be done? The chief strain must undoubtedly be borne by the poor-law, and the poor-law must follow rules—hard-and-fast lines. The simplest rule is indoor relief for all applicants, and if for able-bodied men the relief take the form of work which is educational, its helpfulness will be obvious. The casual labourer, whose family is given necessary support on condition that he enters the House, may, during his residence, learn something of whitewashing, woodwork, and baking, or, better yet, that habit of regularity which will do much to keep up the home which has been kept together for him.

The poor-law can thus help during a time of pressure without any break in its established system. If more is necessary, perhaps the next best form of relief would be an extension of that adopted by the Whitechapel Committee of the Mansion House Fund. By co-operation with other local authorities the guardians might offer more work at street sweeping, or cleaning—which in poor London is never adequately done—under such conditions of residence or providence as would prevent immigration, but would be free of the degrading associations of the stone-yards. The staff at the disposal of the guardians would enable them to try the experiment more effectively than was possible when a voluntary committee without experience, time, or staff had to do everything.

By some such plans relief could be afforded to all who belong to what may be called the lowest class; for the assistance of those who could be helped by tools, emigration, or money, the great Friendly Societies, the Society for Relief of Distress, and the Charity Organisation Society might act in conjunction. These societies are unsectarian, are already organised, and may be developed in power and tenderness to any extent by the addition of members and visitors.

These means and all means which are suggested seem sadly inadequate, and in their very setting forth provoke criticism. There are no effectual means but those which grow in a Christian society. The force which, without striving and crying, without even entering into collision with it, destroyed slavery will also destroy poverty. When rich men, knowing God, realise that life is giving, and when poor men, also knowing God, understand that being is better than having, then there will be none too rich to enter the kingdom of heaven, and none too poor to enjoy God's world.

SAMUEL A. BARNETT.

III.

PASSIONLESS REFORMERS.[1]

THE mention of the poor brings up to most people's minds scenes of suffering, want, and misery. The vast number of people who, while poor in money, are rich in life's good, who live quiet, thoughtful, dignified lives, are forgotten, and the word 'poor' means to many the class which we may call degraded. But the first class is by far the largest, and the wide East End of London (which the indolent think of only as revolting) contains at a rough calculation, say, twenty of the worthy poor to one of the degraded poor. It is curious how widely spread is the reverse idea. Many times have I been asked if I am not 'afraid to walk in East London,' and an article on the People's Entertainment Society aroused, not unjustly, the anger of the East London people at the writer's descriptions of them and of her fears for her personal safety while standing in the Mile End Road! One lady, after a visit to St. George's-in-the-East and Stepney, expressed great astonishment to find that the people lived in *houses*. She had expected that they abode, not exactly in tents, but in huts, old railway carriages, caravans, or squatted

[1] Reprinted, by permission, from the *Fortnightly Review* of August 1882.

against a wall. East Londoners will be glad to know that she went back a wiser and not a sadder woman, having learnt that riches are not necessary to refinement, that some of the noblest characters are developed under the enforced self-control of an income of a pound or thirty shillings a week, that love lived side by side with poverty without thought of exit by the window though poverty had trodden a beaten path through the door, and that books and ideas, though not plentiful enough to become toys, were read, loved, and lived with until they became part of the being of their possessors.

But distinct from this class—among whom may be counted some of the noblest examples of life—there is the class of degraded poor. Here the want is not so much a want of money (some of the trades, such as hawking, flower-selling, shoe-blacking, occasionally bringing in as much as from ten to twenty shillings a day) as the want of the common virtues of ordinary life. In many of these poor, the mere intellectual conception of principle, as such, is absent; they have no moral ideal; spirituality to them is as little understood in idea as in word. Sinning (sensual low brutal sins) is the most common, the to-be-expected course. The standard has got reversed, and those who have turnings towards, and vague aspirations for, better things too often find it impossible to give these feelings practical expression in a society where wrong is upheld by public opinion; where the only test of right is the avoidance of being 'nabbed' by the police; and the highest law is that expressed by the magistrate.

How can these people be raised to enjoy spiritual life? Too often the symptoms are mistaken for the disease. In times of illness, bad weather, or depression of their particular trade, their poverty is the one apparent fact about them, and tender-hearted people rush eagerly to relieve it. That poverty was but the natural result of their sinful, self-indulgent lives; and by it they might have learnt great lessons. The hands of the charity-giver too often, in such cases, act as a screen between a man and his Almighty Teacher. The physical suffering which should have recalled to him his past carelessness or sin is thus made of no avail. Mistaken love! gifts cannot raise these people. Better houses, provident clubs, savings banks, &c. are all useful and do necessary work in forming a good ground in which the seed can grow, but thought must be given lest such efforts leave the people in the condition of more comfortable animals. Materialism is already so strong a force in the world that those who look deeper than the material part of man should beware lest they accentuate what is, in whatever form it appears—whether in the low sensuality of the degraded or the enervating luxury of the æsthete—a circumscribed, ungodly life.

The stimulus of 'getting on' is also used, but it is a dangerous influence, sapping ofttimes the one virtue which is strong and beautiful in the lives of these people, their communistic love; and if adopted by minds empty of principle may become a new source of wrong. 'Getting on' regardless of the means is but another way of going back.

Influences calling themselves religious are tried, and chiefly, all honour be to them, by the evangelicals who, filled with horror at what they hold to be the ultimate fate of such masses, go fearlessly and perseveringly among them, preaching earnestly, if not always rationally, their special tenets. Heaven, as a material place, they still paint in the poetic terms which represented to the Oriental mind the highest spiritual happiness, and is offered as a reward to men imbued with the materialistic spirit of the age, and living coarse and sensual lives. Hell, as a place of physical suffering, is so often threatened that it becomes to many people the most likely thing that they shall go there. The story is perfectly true of the clergyman who, preaching to one of these oft-threatened congregations, tried to show them that sin (according to his explanation removal from God) was hell, and that the awfulness of hell did not consist in being a place where the body would be uncomfortable, but in being a state from which all good and God were absent. Walking behind some of his hearers afterwards, he overheard, ' Parson says there be'ant no hell, Dick. Where be you and I to go then ? ' Imagine feeling homeless because there may be no hell!

But even if the talk of hell still awakens some fear and dread, it is again only a material horror—it but exaggerates the importance of the body, and projects into an after-death sphere the selfish animal life already being led. This will not cultivate spirituality. No! religion thus materialised is a dead-letter; it will not feed the spiritual needs of the people. We have forgotten the words of the Divine Teacher about casting pearls before the swine, and the swine have turned again and rent us. As an old Cornish coachman said the other day in answer to a question about the services of a church which we happened to be passing, ' Ay, yes, there's a great advance in church activity, no doubt of that, but little in spirituality somehow. The people's souls have been preached to death.'

The religionists have taught until the people know all and feel nothing; they have talked about religion till it palls in the hearer's ears. They have blasphemed by asking *pity* for our Lord's physical sufferings when His thoughts and being were at *one* with God; when He was exulting (as only noble souls can faintly conceive of exultation) in His finished work.

Religion has been degraded by these teachers until it is difficult to gain the people's ears to hear it. I have often watched congregations who, keenly interested so long as personal narratives are told, books discussed, or allegories pictured, relax their attention so soon as religion is reverted to, with an air which is told in every muscle of 'knowing all that.' The story once humorously told by the lamented Leonard Montefiore of his experience as a Sabbath-school teacher is a little straw showing withal the way of the stream. Feeling somewhat at a loss as to what to teach, the class being a strange one, he thought he would be safe in telling them a Bible story; so he began on Moses' history, painting, as only he could paint for children's minds, the conditions of the times, making Egypt, with its gorgeous palaces and age-defying temples, live again, showing the princess as a very fairy one, and letting them see through his well-cultivated mind the very age of Rameses. All went well, the children breathless with interest, until he came to the familiar incident of the little ark and the crying babe—'Oh! 'tis only Moses again!' cried one boy, and their interest vanished; they half felt they had been 'taken in,' and for the remainder of the lesson they gave him a bad time.

The experience of many a popular preacher would, if he confessed honestly, be much the same as Mr. Montefiore's. One body of evangelists, in order to attract the people, started a band which, playing loud, blatant marches or swinging hymn tunes, brought hundreds of people, who sat and listened with interest to the music. On its stopping and the preacher rising to speak, the people got up and poured out through the large open gate. The preacher paused, and on a sign the music recommenced and the audience sat down again. Three times was the effort made. No! though the preacher was advertised as the converted swindler or gipsy, or some such attractive title, it was of no avail. The people would not listen to the 'old, old story'—'Bless you, my children,' said he, at last, sitting down in despair, 'but I wish you'd mend yer manners.' It was a larger rent than their manners which wanted mending. These people's lives are already too full of excitement. There is no rest nor repose in them. Dignity has given way to hurry. To attract them to religion, further excitement is often resorted to, and sensationalism with all its vulgarity is brought to play upon the buried soul which we are told we should 'possess in quietness.'

I was once present at a religious meeting where the preacher narrated, with much gusto, accounts of sudden and unexpected deaths and the ultimate fate of the dead ones, making the ignorant audience feel fearful that their every breath might be their last. Finding that even this did not sufficiently stir the people, he pleaded that God in His mercy 'would shut the doors of hell—aye, even with a *bang*!'—for a few moments until he had saved the souls before him. After the word 'bang' he paused in an attitude of attention as if listening to hear the slamming doors. The excitement was intense; many weak-minded people went into hysterics and others hastened to be converted and 'made safe' while the hell-doors were shut. To such means have some religionists reverted to teach the people the Gospel!

No, alas! the old channels are no longer available for the water of life; without it the people are dead, live they ever so comfortably. A spiritual life is the true life; as men become spiritualised, as the moral ideal becomes the source of action, the old words and forms may regain meaning. Phrases now to them meaning nothing or only superstition will then express their very being; but without a belief in the ideal they are but empty words, like 'the sounding brass or tinkling cymbal.'

How can these degraded people be given these priceless gifts? The usual religious means have failed, the unusual must be tried; we must deal with the people as individuals, being content to speak, not to the thousands, but to ones and twos; we must become the friend, the intimate of a few; we must lead them up through the well-known paths of cleanliness, honesty, industry, until we attain the higher ground whence glimpses can be caught of the brighter land, the land of spiritual life.

Hitherto the large number of the degraded people have appalled the philanthropist; they have been spoken of as the 'lapsed masses'; and efforts to reach them have not been considered successful unless the results can be counted by hundreds. But there is the higher authority for the individual teaching; He whom all men now delight to honour, whose life, words, and actions are held up for imitation; He chose twelve only to especially influence; He spent long hours in conversation with single persons; He thought no incident too trivial to inquire into, no petty quarrel beneath His interference. We must know and be known, love and be loved, by our less happy brother until he learn, through the friend whom he has seen, knowledge of God whom he has not seen. All this must be done, and not one stone of practical helpfulness left unturned, and

> God's passionless reformers, influences
> That purify and heal and are not seen,

must be summoned also to give their aid. Among these are flowers, not given in bundles nor loose, but daintily arranged in bouquets, brought by the hand of the friend who will stop to carefully dispose them in the broken jug or cracked basin, so that they should lose none of their beauty as long as the close atmosphere allows them to live: flowers (without text-cards) left to speak their own message, allowed to tell the story of perfect work without speech or language; all the better preachers because so lacking in self-consciousness.

Not second among such reformers may be placed high-class music, both instrumental and vocal, given in schoolrooms, mission-rooms, and, if possible, in churches where the traditions speak of worship, where the atmosphere is prayerful, and where the arrangement of the seats suggests kneeling; just the music without a form of service, nor necessarily an address, only a hymn sung in unison and a blessing from the altar at the close. To hear oratorios—*St. Paul*, the *Messiah*, *Elijah*, Spohr's *Last Judgment*—I have seen crowds of the lowest class, some shoeless and bonnetless, and all having the 'savour of the great unwashed,' sit in church for two hours at a time quietly and reverently, the long lines of seated folk being now and then broken by a kneeling figure, driven to his knees by the glorious burst of sound which had awakened strange emotions; while the almost breathless silence in the solos has been occasionally interrupted by a heart-drawn sigh.

To trace the result is impossible and not advisable; but who can doubt that in those moments, brief as they were, the curtain of the flesh was raised and the soul became visible, perhaps by the discovery startling its possessor into new aspirations?

One man came after such a service for help, not money help, but because he was a drunkard, saying if 'I could hear music like that every night I should not need the drink.' It was but a feeble echo of St. Paul's words, 'Who can deliver me from the body of this death?' a cry—a prayer—which given to music might be borne by the sweet messenger through heaven's gate to the very throne beyond.

Then there are country visits; quiet afternoons in the country, not 'treats' where numbers bring wild excitement, and only the place, not the sort of amusement, is changed; but where a few people spend an afternoon quietly in the country, perhaps entertained at tea by a kindly friend; parties at which there is time to *feel* the quiet; where the moments are not so full of external and active interests that there is no opportunity to 'possess the soul'; parties at which there is a possibility of 'hush,' in which, helped by Nature's ritual, perfect in sound, scent, and colour, silent worship can go on.

For people spending long years in the close courts and streets of ugly towns, the mere sight of nature is startling, and may awaken longings, to themselves strange, to others indescribable, but which are the stirrings of the life within.

The stories of great lives, and of other religions, very simply told, as far as possible leaving out the foreign conditions which confuse the ignorant mind, are sometimes helpful. It is generally considered wise to hide from children and untutored people the knowledge of other religions, for fear it should awaken doubts concerning their own; but in those cases where their own is so very negative, it is often helpful to learn of faiths held by the large masses of mankind. To hear that the great fundamental ideas of all worships are similar would perhaps suggest to the hearer that there might be more in it than 'just parson stuff' and lead him to inquire further; or, if it did not do this, it would be some gain to remove the ignorance which, more than familiarity, breeds contempt of the despised foreigner.

Once, after a talk about Egypt and its old religion, the Osiris worship, the beautiful story of the virgin Isis, and her son Horus, who was slain by Set, the King of Evil, and rose again from the bosom of the Nile, I heard it said, 'They thought the same then, did they? only called them different names.' The largeness of the idea caught the hearer; its universality bore testimony to its truth. Would it not be helpful if our religious teachers, instead of spending their precious time denouncing the errors of other religions, would take the truths running through the great stories common to them all, and in an historical attitude of mind show the growth of thought, the development of spirituality till his hearers are brought face to face with the Founder of our religion, who set the noblest example; taught the purest doctrine; lived the highest spiritual life; was in Himself, to use the Bible words, 'the way, the truth, and the life'?

Again, to be quiet, to be alone are among influences that purify. Every one when abroad has, I suppose, felt the privilege of being able to go into the churches whenever they wished. In our great towns the privilege is equally needed, and, where the poor live, doubly so. When one room has to be shared by the whole family, sometimes including a lodger, there can be no quiet, and loneliness is impossible. Some of the clergy are recognising this want, and open their churches at other than service times, but the practice is still rare. A notice outside our church tells how those may enter who 'wish to think or pray in quietness.' About ten a day use the permission, some of them kneeling shyly in the side aisle, as if their attitude were unwonted and caused shame; others sitting quietly for a long time, as if weary of the grind and noise outside; while sometimes men come to make their mid-day prayer. Here again is a means with invisible results; but quiet and loneliness are possessions to which every one has a right, without which it is difficult, almost impossible, to 'commune with God,' and the gift of which is still to be given to the poor.

Then there is the beauty of Art, now almost entirely

absent from the dwellings of the poor, and yet by them so felt as a pleasure; the beauty of form and colour, which it is possible to show in schoolroom and church decoration; the beauty of light and brightness, the beauty of growth to be seen in gardens and churchyards. Outside our church are planted two Virginia creepers; poor things they are, hardly to be recognised by their relations in kindlier soil. But once, in a third-class carriage, I was surprised to hear the church described as the one 'where the jennies growed.'

It is easier now (thanks to the Kyrle Society and Miss Harrison's generous gifts of work) to make school and mission rooms pretty. A beautiful workroom is a very strong, though invisible, influence. One girl, who had to leave our school on account of moving from the neighbourhood, said quite naturally, among her regrets at leaving and her description of the new school, 'It is so ugly it makes one not care.'

The pictures in a schoolroom should be various, and, if possible, often changed. Pictures of action or of historical incidents are the most generally appreciated, but pictures of flowers, fairy tales, landscapes, and sea are suggestive.

Picture galleries have hitherto been thought of chiefly as pleasure places for the educated, or as schools for the student. They can become mission-halls for the degraded. It is easy to arrange visits with a few people to the National Gallery, to the Kensington or Bethnal Green Museums; it is not an unpleasant afternoon's work to guide little groups of people, just pointing out this beautiful picture, or putting in a few words to explain this or that historical allusion. I once took a girl

—a merry lassie, light-hearted, fond of pleasure, but in danger of taking it at the expense of her character—to the National Gallery. The little picture of Raphael's, where the women acting as the angels stand over the sleeping knight, offering him the protecting shield, opened to her a new truth. Here was a fresh possible relation between man and woman, not the one of rough jokes and doubtful fun, but a new connection not to be despised, either, where the province of the woman was to keep the man safe; a large lesson taught by dumb lips and dead hands.

When Sir Richard Wallace lent his pictures to the Bethnal Green Museum, he not only brightened the eyes of many used only to the drear monotony of East London, but he taught one poor wretched woman with a whining baby hanging on her thin breast a large lesson. Dirt on child and mother showed her condition, and was a dreary contrast to the Madonna with lovely crowing baby before whom the little group paused. 'Ah, yer could easy enough "mother" such a baby as that now,' was her apologetic remark, showing that the picture had conveyed the rebuke, and that the reverence born of faith in the painter's heart had not yet finished bearing fruit.

It is but feebly that I have tried to show how such means could be used to teach spirituality to the lowest classes. It is not necessary to speak of school-lessons, lending libraries, mothers' meetings, night-schools, temperance societies, and clubs; agencies for the good of the people which are at work in every well-organised parish; neither has mention been made of the communicants' meetings, prayer assemblies, church services, which are food to feed and build up many of those who already recognise their true life, and strive bravely, amid adverse circumstances, to live it. We can all work at these in gladness and thanksgiving. They are not so hard to persevere with, for some result attends them. In meetings and classes there is encouragement in the regularity and the appreciation of the attendants. In services and prayer-meetings there is the knowledge that they help and strengthen the faint-hearted; but in the indirect means of helping the degraded there is little encouragement, for there can be no results. The highest work is often apparently resultless, bringing no personal thanks, no world's applause; a failure, worthless labour, if judged by the world's standard of work; a success, worth doing, if it open to a few, whom the usual means have failed to reach, the great secret of true being, their spiritual life; a buried life, buried but not dead.

HENRIETTA O. BARNETT.

IV.

TOWN COUNCILS AND SOCIAL REFORM.[1]

Mr. BRIGHT has stated that in Glasgow 41,000 families occupy single rooms. The statement caused no surprise to those familiar with the poor quarters of our great towns; their surprise has been that the statement should cause surprise in any section of the community. It is, indeed, surprising that people should think so little about what they daily see, and should go on talking as if 20s. or 30s. a week were enough to satisfy the needs of a family's life, and should be surprised that many persons still occupy one room, endure hardship and die, killed by the struggle to exist. It is surprising that reflection on such subjects is not more common because, when facts are stated, no defence is made for the present condition of the people.

Alongside of the growth of wealth during this age there has been growth of the belief in the powers of human nature, of the belief that in all men, independent of rank and birth, there exist great powers of being. 'Nothing can breed such awe and fear as fall upon us when we look into our minds, into the mind of man,' expresses the experience of many who do not use the poet's words.

[1] Reprinted, by permission, from the *Nineteenth Century* of November 1883.

Those who are conscious of what men may be and do cannot be satisfied while the majority of Englishmen live, in the midst of wealthy England, stinted and joyless lives because they are poor.

When facts, therefore, such as that referred to by Mr. Bright are stated, no defence is made; and such facts are common. Here are some :—(1) The death-rate among the children of the poor is double that among the children of the rich. Born in some small room, which serves as the sleeping and living room of the family; hushed to sleep by discordant noises from neighbouring factories, refreshed by air laden with smoke and evil odours, forced to find their play in the streets; without country holiday or adequate medical skill, without sufficient air, space, or water, the children die, and the mothers among the poor are always weeping for their children and cannot be comforted. (2) The occupants of the prisons are mostly of one class—the poor. The fact for its explanation needs no assumption that 'the poor in a lump are bad'; it is the natural result of their condition. It is because children are ill developed or unhealthily developed by life in the streets that they become idlers, sharpers, or thieves. It is because families are crowded together that quarrels begin and end in fights. It is because they have not the means to hide their vices under respectable forms that the poor go to prison and not the rich. (3) The lives of the people are joyless. The slaves of toil, worn by anxiety lest the slavery should end, they have not leisure nor calm for thought; they cannot therefore be happy, living in the thought of other times, as those are happy who, in reading or travel, have gathered memories to be the bliss of solitude, or as those who, 'by discerning intellect,' have found the best to be 'the simple product of the common day.' When work ceases, the one resource is excitement; and thus their lives are joyless. Anxiety consumes their powers in pleasure as in work, the faces of the women lose their beauty, and a woman of thirty looks old.

These are facts patent to those who know our great towns—the facts of life, not among a few of their degraded inhabitants, but facts of the life of the majority of the people. Let any one who does not know how his neighbours live set himself the following sum. Given 20s. or 40s. a week wages, how to keep a family, pay rent of 2s. 6d. a week for each room, and lay up an adequate amount for times of bad trade, sickness, and old age. As the sum is worked out, as it is seen how one after another the things which seem to make life worth living have to be given up, and as it is seen how many 'necessaries' are impossible, how many of the poor must put up with a diet more scanty than that allowed to paupers, how all must go without the leisure and the knowledge which transmute existence into life—faith will be shaken in many theories of social reform.

Teetotal advocates will preach in vain that drunkenness is the root of all evil, and that a nation of abstainers will be either a healthy, a happy, or a thoughtful nation. Thrift will be seen to be powerless to do more than to create a smug and transient respectability, and even those who are 'converted' will not claim to be raised by their faith out of the reach of early death and poverty into a life which belongs to their nature as members in the human family.

Theories of reform which do not touch the conditions

in which the people live, which do not make possible for them fuller lives in happier circumstances, are not satisfactory. The conversion of sinners—at any rate while the sinners are sought chiefly among the poor—the emigration of children, the spread of thrift and temperance among the workpeople, will still leave families occupying single rooms and the sons of men the joyless slaves of work; a state of society for which no defence can be made.

It is only a larger share of wealth which can increase comfort and relieve men from the pressure brought on them by the close atmosphere of great towns; which can, in a word, give to all the results of thought and open to all the life which is possible. If it be that the return for fair land laid waste by mines and engines is wider knowledge of men and things, it is only the rich who now enjoy this return and it is only wealth which can make it common. And since any distribution of wealth in the shape of money relief would be fatal to the independence of the people, the one satisfactory method of social reform is that which tends to make more common the good things which wealth has gained for the few. The nationalisation of luxury must be the object of social reformers.

The presence of wealth is so obvious that the attempts to distribute its benefits both by individuals and by societies have been many. Individuals have given their money and their time; their failure is notorious, and societies have been formed to direct their efforts. The failure of these societies is not equally notorious, but few thinkers retain the hope that societies will reform Society and make the conditions of living such that people will be able to grow in wisdom and in stature to

F

the full height of their manhood. If it were a sight to make men and angels weep to see one rich man struggling with the poverty of a street, making himself poor only to make others discontented paupers, it is as sad a sight to see societies hopelessly beaten and hardened into machines with no 'reach beyond their grasp.' The deadness of these societies or their ill-directed efforts has roused in the shape of Charity Organisation workers a most striking missionary enterprise. The history of the movement as a mission has yet to be written; the names of its martyrs stand in the list of the unknown good; but the most earnest member of a Charity Organisation Society cannot hope that organised almsgiving will be powerful so to alter conditions as to make the life of the poor a life worth living.

Societies which absorb much wealth, and which relieve their subscribers of their responsibility, are failing; it remains only to adopt the principle of the Education Act, of the Poor Law, and of other socialistic legislation, and call on Society to do what societies fail to do. There is much which may be urged in favour of such a course. It is only Society, or, to use the title by which Society expresses itself in towns, it is only Town Councils, which can cover all the ground and see that each locality gets equal treatment. It is by common action that a healthy spirit becomes common, and the tone of public opinion may be more healthy when the Town Council engages in good-doing than when good-doing is the monopoly of individuals or of societies. If nations have been ennobled by wars undertaken against an enemy, towns may be ennobled by work undertaken against the evils of poverty.

Through the centuries the sense of the duties of Society has been growing. Some earnest men may regret the limit placed on individual action and the failure of societies, but the change they regret is more apparent than real. The Town Councils are, indeed, the modern representatives of the Church and of other societies, through which in older times individuals expressed their hope and work, and to these bodies falls the duty of effecting that social reform which will help the poor to grow to the stature of the life of men.

The problem before them is one much more of ways than of means. If poverty is depressing the lives of the people, the wealth by which it may be relieved is superabundant. On the one side, there is disease for the want of food and doctors; on the other side there is disease because of food and doctors. In one part of the town the women cease to charm for want of finery; in the other they cease to please from excess of finery. It is for want of money that the streets in which the poor live are close, ill-swept, and ill-lighted; that the 'East Ends' of towns have no grand meeting-rooms and no beauty. It is through superfluity of money that the entertainments of the rich are made tiresome with music, and their picture galleries made ugly with uninteresting portraits. There is no want of means for making better the condition of the people; and there has ever been sufficient good-will to use the means when the way has been clear. To discover the way is the problem of the times.

Some way must be found which, without pauperising, without affecting the spirit of energy and independence, shall give to the inhabitants of our great towns the surroundings which will increase joy and develop life.

The first need is better dwellings. While the people live without adequate air, space, or light in houses where the arrangements are such that privacy is impossible, it is hopeless to expect that they will enjoy the best things. The need has been recognised, and, happily without going to Parliament, Town Councils may do much to meet the need. It is in their power to enforce sanitary improvements, to make every house healthy and clean, and to provide common rooms which will serve as libraries or drawing-rooms. If it is not in their power to reduce rents, it is possible for them to pull down unfit buildings, and sell the ground to builders at a low price, on condition that such builders shall provide extra appliances for the health and pleasure of the people.

Insanitary conditions and high rents are the points to which consideration must be directed. Builders to-day build houses on the fiction that each house will be occupied by one family. The fact that two or three families will at once take possession is kept out of sight, while the parlour, drawing-room, and single set of offices are finished off to suit the requirements of an English home. The fiction ends in the creation of evils on which medical officers write reports, and of other evils which, like Medusa's head, are best seen by the shadow they cast on Society.

The insanitary conditions constitute one difficulty connected with the dwellings of the poor; the rent for adequate accommodation which absorbs one quarter of an irregular income constitutes another. To cure the insanitary conditions ample power exists; to even suggest a means for lowering rents is not so easy. Perhaps it might be possible for the community to sell the ground it acquires at some low price, on condition that the rents of the newly built houses should never exceed a certain rate, and that the occupier should always have the right of purchase. Such a condition is not, however, at present legal, and is of doubtful expediency. It is now possible for Town Councils to acquire land under the Artisans' Dwellings Act, and to sell it cheaply on condition that the rooms are of a certain size and provided with certain appliances; that special arrangements are made for washing and cleaning, and that a common room is at the disposal of a certain number of families.

The improvement cannot be made without what is called a loss—that is to say, the Town Councils cannot sell land for the building of fit dwellings at the same price for which the land had been acquired. Money will in one sense be lost; and this phrase has such power that, though the need is recognised, the Act by which the need could be met has in most towns remained a dead letter. In Liverpool, where, according to official reports, the state of the dwellings is productive of fever and destructive of common decency, the Act has never been applied. In Manchester, where it is acknowledged to be the object of the Town Council to protect the health of the people, it is stated in the last report that the Act involves too great an outlay to be workable. The London Metropolitan Board of Works, which spends its millions wisely and unwisely, has striven to show that the application of the Act would lay too great a burden on the ratepayers. It is impossible, it is said, to house the poor at such a cost. It would not seem impossible if it were recognised that to spend money in housing the poor is a way of making the wealth of the town serve the needs of the town. It would not seem impossible if Town Councils recognised that on them has come the care of the people, and that money is not lost which is returned in longer and better life.

Other needs exist, hardly second to that of better dwellings, and these it is in the power of local authorities to meet, in a way of which few reformers seem to be aware. The Town Councils may provide means of recreation and instruction—libraries, playgrounds, and public baths. School Boards may provide, not only elementary instruction, but give a character to education, and use their buildings as centres for the meetings, classes, and recreation of the old scholars. Boards of Guardians may make their relief, not only a means of meeting destitution, but a means of educating the independence of the strong and of comforting the sorrows of the weak. We can imagine these boards, the councils of the town, endowed with greater powers; but with those they already possess they could change the social conditions and remove abuses for which Englishmen make no defence.

Wise Town Councils, conscious of the mission they have inherited, could destroy every court and crowded alley and put in their places healthy dwellings; they could make water so cheap and bathing-places so common that cleanliness should no longer be a hard virtue; they could open playgrounds, and take away from a city the reproach of its gutter-children; they could provide gardens, libraries, and conversation-rooms, and make the pleasures of intercourse a delight to the poor, as it is a delight to the rich; they could open picture galleries and concerts, and give to all that pleasure which comes as surely from a common as from a private possession; they could light and clean the streets of the poor quarters; they could stamp out disease, and by enforcing regulations against smoke and all uncleanness limit the destructiveness of trade and lengthen the span of life; they could empty the streets of the boys and girls, too big for the narrow homes, too small for the clubs and public-houses, by opening for them playrooms and gymnasia; they could help the strong and hopeful to emigrate; they could give medicine to heal the sick, money to the old and poor, a training for the neglected, and a home for the friendless.

With this power in the hands of Town Councils, and with our great towns in such a state that a fact as to their condition shocks the nation, there is no need to wait for parliamentary action. The course on which the authorities are asked to enter is no untried one.

There are local bodies which have applied the Artisans' Dwellings Act and cleared away houses or hovels, of which the medical officers' descriptions are not fit for repetition in polite society. There are those who have built, and more who are ready to build, houses which shall at any rate give the people healthy surroundings, possibilities of home life and of common pleasures, even when a family can afford only a single room. And, although the London School Board's buildings and playgrounds are occupied only during a few hours in each week, there are schools which are used for meetings, for classes in higher education, and for Art Exhibitions, and there are playgrounds which are open all day and every day to all comers. The way in which Guardians have in some unions made the system of relief in the highest sense educational is now an old tale. It has been shown that out-relief, with its demoralising results, may be abolished; it is being shown that a workhouse with trade masters and 'mental instructors' may be a reformatory; and it is not beyond the hope of some Boards that a system of medical relief may be developed adequate to the needs of the people. Public bodies here and there are showing what it is in their power to do, but at present their efforts hardly make any mark; they must become general.

The first practical work is to rouse the Town Councils to the sense of their powers; to make them feel that their reason of being is not political but social, that their duty is not to protect the pockets of the rich, but to save the people. It is for reformers in every town to direct all their force on the Town Councils, to turn aside to no scheme, and to start no new society, but to urge, in season and out of season, that the care of the people is the care of the community, and not of any philanthropic section—is, indeed, the care of Society, and not of societies. 'The People, not Politics,' should be their cry; and they should see that the power is in the hands of men, irrespective of party or of class, who care for the people. This is the first practical work, one in which all can join, whether he serves as elector or elected. It may be that efficient administration will show that without an increase of rating a sufficient fund may be found to do all that needs doing; but, if this is not the case, the social interest which is aroused will act on Parliament, and that body will be diverted from its party politics to consider how, by some change in taxation, by progressive rating, by a land-tax, or by some other means, the money can be raised to do what must be done.

The means, I repeat, is a matter for the future; the battle is to be won at the municipal elections; it is there the cry 'The People, not Politics' must be raised, and it is the councils of the town which can work the social reform. If it be urged that when Town Councils do for social reform all which can be done, the condition will still be unsatisfactory, I agree. Wealth cannot supply the needs of life, and many who have all that wealth can give are still without the life which is possible to men. The town in which houses shall be good, health general, and recreation possible, may be but a whited sepulchre. No social reform will be adequate which does not touch social relations, bind classes by friendship, and pass, through the medium of friendship, the spirit which inspires righteousness and devotion.

If, therefore, the first practical work of reformers be to rouse Town Councils, their second is to associate volunteers who will work with the official bodies. We may here regret the absence of a truly National Church. If in every parish Church Boards existed representative of every religious opinion and expressive of every form of philanthrophy, they would be the centres round which such volunteers would gather and prove themselves to be an agency ready to their hand. While we hope for such boards there is no need to wait to act.

As a rule, it may be laid down that the voluntary work is most effective when it is in connection with official work. The connection gives a backbone, a dignity to work, which has lost something in the hands of Sunday-school teachers and district visitors. In every town volunteers in connection with official work are wanted. It is doubtful, indeed, if the tenements occupied by the least instructed classes could be kept in order, or the people made to live up to their better surroundings, if the rent collecting were not put in the hands of volunteers with the time to make friends and the will to have patience with the tenants. At any rate, wherever official work is done there will be something for volunteers to supply.

Guardians want those who will consider the poor; men who will visit the workhouse to rouse those too idle or too depressed to work, and to find help for those who by sickness or ill-chance have lost their footing in the rush for living. They want those who, knowing what wages can do and cannot do, will serve on relief committees, will see the poor in their distress, and, giving or not giving, will try to make them understand that care does not cease. They want also women who will be friends to the sick and, more than that, befriend the girls who drift wretched to the workhouse, or go out lonely from the pauper schools. School Boards want those who, visiting the schools, will seek out the children who are fit for country holidays, visit the homes, and do something to follow up the education between the years of thirteen and twenty-one.

Wherever there is an institution, a reading-room, a club, or a playground there is work for volunteers. It may not be that the volunteers will seem to do much; they will be certain to do something. They will be certain to make links between the classes, and lead both rich and poor to give up habits which keep them apart. They will be certain to add strength to the public opinion, which by the bye will relieve those whose higher life is destroyed by excess or by want. They will be certain to do something, and if they carry into their work a spirit of devotion, a faith in the high calling of the human race, and a love for its weakest members, there is no limit which can be placed on what they will do. They will put into the sound body the sound mind; into the well-ordered town citizens who ' feel deep, think clear, and bear fruit well.'

SAMUEL A. BARNETT.

V.

'AT HOME' TO THE POOR.[1]

Few people realise the extreme dulness of the lives of the poor. Cut off from the many interests which education or the possession of money gives, they have little left but the 'trivial round, the common task,' which indeed furnishes them with ' room to deny themselves,' but is hardly, in their case at least, ' the road to bring them daily nearer God.'

'People must be amuthed,' is the caricatured statement of a true human need, and the terrible and often deplored attraction of the public-house has its root not so much in the love of strong drink as in the want of interest and desire for amusement felt by the lower classes of the poor. This is especially true with regard to the women and to those men who cannot read. Unable to comprehend the ever-living interest of watching public affairs, prevented by ignorance from following, even in outline, the actions of the nations, they are thrown back on the affairs of their neighbours, and centre all their interest in the sayings and doings of quarrelsome Mr. Jones or much-abused Mrs. Smith.

It is difficult for those of us to whom the world seems almost too full of interests to realise the deadening dul-

---

[1] Reprinted, by permission, from the *Cornhill Magazine* of May 1881.

ness of some of these lives. Let us imagine, for an instant, all knowledge of history, geography, art, science, and language blotted out; all interests in politics, social movements, and discoveries obliterated; no society pleasures to anticipate; no trials of skill nor tests of proficiency in work or play to look forward to; no money at command to enable us to plan some pleasure for a friend or dependent; no books always at hand, the old friends waiting silently till their acquaintance is renewed, the new ones standing ready to be learnt and loved; no opportunities of getting change of scene and idea; no memories laden with pleasures of travel; no objects of real beauty to look at. What would our lives become? And yet this is a true picture of the lives of thousands of the poorer classes, whose time is passed in hard, monotonous work, or occupied in the petty cares of many children, and in satisfying the sordid wants of the body. In some cases precarious labour adds the element of uncertainty to the other troubles, an element which, by the fact of its bringing some interest, is enjoyed by the men, but which adds tenfold to the many cares of the housewife.

It is not easy to see how the poor themselves can get out of this atmosphere of dulness. They can hardly give parties, even if the cost of entertaining were not a sufficient barrier; the extreme smallness of the rooms entirely prevents social intercourse, not to mention the hindrance caused by the necessity for putting the children to bed in the course of the evening, and by all the many discomforts consequent on the one room being bedroom, parlour, kitchen, and scullery. But even supposing there are two rooms, or few children, the difficulties of entertaining are not yet over. With minds so barren, conversation can hardly be the source of much amusement, and music and dancing are almost impossible with no instrument to help and no space where even the little feet can patter.

But it is possible for the ignorant as well as the cultured to enjoy Nature. And it is often a subject of wonder why the poor living in such close streets or alleys, surrounded with such unlovely objects, do not take more trouble to get out into the country or enjoy the parks. 'Only sixpence, you say,' said a hard-working pale body to me one day when I was urging her to go on one of her enforced idle afternoons to get air and see some refreshing beauty at Hampstead. 'Well, yer see, I could hardly go without the three children, and that's 1s. 3d.; besides they'd be a deal hungrier when they came home than perhaps I could manage for.'

What could be said to the last argument? Just fancy having to consider, otherwise than pleasurably, the increased appetite of one of our young ones fresh from a day by the sea or in the country?

But, apart from the money question, the desire to go into the country after a time wears off, even among those who have before lived in pure air and among country sights and scenes; people get used to their dull, sordid surroundings; the memory of fairer sights grows dim, and the imagination is not strong enough to conjure them up again.

'Shure, I ain't been in the country this fifteen year,' an old woman once startled me by saying at a country party; 'and if it hadn't been for your note 'ere it would ha' been another fifteen year afore I'd ha' seen it.'

And she was not so poor, this old lady; 7*s*. a week, perhaps, and 2*s*. 6*d*. to pay for rent. It was not her poverty which prevented her seeing the fifteen fair springs which had passed since she came from the Green Isle. No! it was just the want of power to make the effort—a loss to her far more serious than the loss of the sight of the country. As the late James Hinton used to say, 'The worst thing is to be in hell and not know it is hell'; perhaps the best thing one can do for another is to give him the glimpse of heaven, which, letting in the light, shows the blackness of hell.

'Don't you think green is God's favourite colour?' asked an old lady, the thought being suggested as we stood together in a forest of soft green. 'Well, I can't say,' was the answer; 'look at the sky; how blue that is.' 'Yes, but that isn't always blue, and the earth is 'most always green.'

Does it not seem a pity that this old poet soul, so fit to teach God's lessons, should live all through the summer days in one room, shared by four other people, seeing only the mud colours of London, which certainly are not God's favourite colours. It was this same old lady who said on receiving her first invitation, 'All the years I've lived in London I was never asked to go into the country before you asked me.'

But the want of pleasure and change is no newly discovered need of the poor. School-treats and excursions and bean-feasts have been organised and carried out almost since Sunday-schools have existed and congregations had a corporate life. Every summer sees the columns of the newspapers used to ask for money to give 900, 1,000, 2,000 children 'one day in the country,' and when the money is obtained and the day arrives, the children are packed into vans or a special train and turned into the woods or fields to enjoy themselves (and tease the frogs) until tea, buns, and hymns bring the ' 'appy day' to an end. Good days these, full of pleasure and health-giving exercise, but perhaps mixed with too large an element of excitement to teach the children to enjoy the country for its own sake, to enable them to learn in Dame Nature's lap ' that we can feed this mind of ours in a wise passiveness.'

Neither have the clergy overlooked this need as existing among their grown people, and most of those working in poor neighbourhoods organise an annual 'Treat,' each person paying, say, 1s., to be met by the 6d. from the Pastor's Fund. These treats sometimes assume the enormous proportions of 2,000 or 3,000 persons. All carry their mid-day meal to be eaten when and how they like. The assembling for tea and a few speeches by the rector and those in authority are the only means taken to bring the people together and to introduce the sense of host and guest. And with the memory of the 1s. paid, this sense is very difficult either to arouse or maintain. But, good as in many ways these treats are, they do not do all they might. They do not introduce fresh experiences, an acquaintance with other lives, the interest of new knowledge.

> We receive but what we give,
> And in our life alone does nature live,

as Coleridge puts it; and such sadly empty minds want the interpretation of the friendly eye to make them see what they went out 'for to see.'

Struck with these ideas, we determined to try another

method of entertaining our neighbours; and believing that they had the same need of social intercourse as that felt by the rich, and taking for granted that the kind of country entertainment most prevalent among the rich was that most enjoyed, we based our parties on the same foundation, remembering always that the minds of the poor being emptier, more active entertainment was needed, and that the party to which we invited them was perhaps the one day's outing in the whole year, the one glimpse that they had (apart from divorce suits) into the lives and habits of the richer classes.

On talking over our plan with friends who, living in the suburbs of London, had the necessary garden, it was not long before we received kindly invitations to take thirty, forty, fifty, of our neighbours to spend the afternoon in the country. The day and hour fixed, it was left with us to decide which guests should be invited, and to pass on the invitation. Sometimes our hosts particularly wish to entertain children as well as grown people; and if so, we include the children in the invitation; but on the whole, experience has taught that those parties are most thoroughly enjoyed from which the children are omitted. This will not be misunderstood when it is remembered that these mothers and fathers have their children, perhaps seven, all small together, constantly with them for 365 days in the year, both day and night; that the children become noisy and excited in the country, and that each child's noise, though it may be music in the ear of its mother, can hardly be anything but what it is, *disagreeable sounds*, in the ears of its mother's neighbour. Another objection to the presence of the children is the extreme difficulty of entertaining them and the grown people together. To the social gatherings of other classes it is not the rule to invite children with their parents, and the taste or feeling which forbids such a rule is common to the poor.

It is not difficult, knowing many people who would be glad of a day's outing, to pass on such invitations; but it is pleasanter, if it can be so arranged, that the guests should beforehand be acquainted with each other. For that reason it is better to invite together the members of a mothers' meeting and their husbands, the *habitués* of a club, the inhabitants of one block of buildings, the denizens of a particular court, the singing-class, the members of any society who worship, work, or learn together—in short, those who unite for any purpose.

There are other advantages in this plan besides the obvious one of the guests being already acquainted. Those who have hitherto seen each other's character from the work point of view only now get another standpoint, and the day's pleasure, together with the hearty laugh and the many-voiced songs, does more than many a pastoral address can do to teach forgiveness and break down barriers raised by quarrels—quarrels which more often owe their origin to close neighbourhoods than to bad tempers. 'Now she ain't such a bad 'un as one would think, considering the way she behaved to my Billy—is she now?' is a true remark illustrating what I would say.

The guests chosen, the invitations go out in the usual form: 'Mrs. So-and-So,' mentioning our hostess's name, 'hopes to have the pleasure of seeing Mr. and Mrs. So-and-So on Monday, 14th, to spend the afternoon in the country,' and then follow the time of the train and the name of the station where the rendezvous is to be held.

Added to these the friends connected in any way with the expected guests, the district visitor, the superintendent of the mothers' meeting, the lady rent-collector are also invited; as well as those who have gifts of entertaining or those to whom we wish to introduce our neighbours. A train is generally chosen between one and two o'clock, so as to enable the man to get a half-day's work and the woman to see to necessary household duties and give the children their dinner before she starts.

On reaching the country station the party rambles through the lanes, picking grasses and flowers, taking, if possible, a détour before arriving at the host's house. 'Why, the *trees* smell,' exclaimed one town-bred woman in almost awe-struck astonishment, standing under a lilac-tree. 'Don't it make one feel gentle-like!' was another remark made more to himself than to anyone else, which came from a rough one-legged board-man, as he stood overlooking a quiet, far-stretching scene near Wimbledon.

Unless one has lived in close streets and amid noise and grinding hurry, it is difficult to understand the pleasures of these walks. The sweetness of the air, the quiet which can be felt, the very fact of strolling in the road without looking out to avoid being run over, are a relief, and the absence of the ever-present anxiety of the care of the children is a great addition to the irresponsible enjoyment of the day.

The destination reached, it is a great help if the host and hostess will come out to meet and welcome the party, as is customary towards guests of other classes. By this simple courtesy the tone is at once given, and the people feel themselves not brought out to a 'treat' but invited and welcomed as guests. I have seen men, among whom we were told when we first went to Whitechapel it was not 'safe' to go alone, entirely changed by the bearing of their hosts to them, and the determination with which they set out, to have a 'lark,' at whatever inconvenience to others, gradually melt away under the influence of being treated as gentlemen. 'Why, she said she was glad to see me,' said a low, coarse fellow, taking as a personal compliment to himself the conventional form of expression.

The duty of introducing and welcoming over, we are glad if we find tables on a shady lawn or under a tent ready spread and waiting for us. In the excitement of getting off, the midday meal taken hurriedly has probably been a slight one, and the walk and unwonted fresh air have given good appetites. Sometimes our hostess has made arrangements that all the party should take their food together, and this is the better plan if it can be managed. 'Why, the gentry is sitting down with us. Now I do call *that* comfortable like,' was overheard on one occasion when this arrangement had been followed. If the one class waits on the other it but emphasises the painful class distinctions so sadly prominent in the ordinary affairs of life, and the feeling aroused in the minds of the people as they see the richer members of the party taken by the hostess to the house to have 'something to eat' is not always amiable, the 'something' being interpreted as better, anyhow other than that provided for them, or why should it not have been taken together?

The repast given by our many kindly hosts during

these eight summers of parties has been various. Some add eggs and bacon to the tea and cakes; others give a large joint, which is even more enjoyed, a cut off a good 14 lb. sirloin of beef being a rare luxury in the ordinary dietary of the working classes, while others again offer tea, differing only in quantity from the ordinary afternoon meal which is commonly taken between lunch and dinner. Some of our hosts give every variety of cake, such as Scotch housewives delight in making, though I remember one lady who, while most kind and anxious to give pleasure, told me, as if it were an additional advantage, that she had 'had all the cakes made very plain, and that they were all baked the day before yesterday.'

The meal over, the real pleasure of the day begins, and this must entirely depend on the capabilities of the hostess for entertaining and on the possibilities of the garden. If it is large, there is nothing townpeople like better than to saunter about, to wander in the shrubberies, to see the hothouses, conservatories, ferneries, especially if some one will be the guide and point out what is interesting, this spot where the best view is to be obtained, that curious flower, and tell the story hanging on this queerly shaped tree. 'Aye, aye, ma'am, it's all very beautiful, but to my mind you're the beautifullest flower of the lot,' was the spontaneous compliment elicited from a weather-beaten costermonger to the stately old lady who had taken pains to show him her garden, and though the remark was greeted with shouts of laughter from the surrounding group, the 'Well, he ain't far wrong, I'm sure,' showed that the words had only spoken out the thoughts of many.

Sometimes the men go off to play cricket or bowls, to

see the puppies or horses, or some other beasts particularly interesting to the masculine mind ; or perhaps the interminable game of rounders occupies all the time. Sometimes swings, see-saws, or a row on the pond are great amusements. 'Oh dear, I think I've only just learnt to enjoy myself,' gasped one buxom woman of fifty, breathless with swinging her neighbour, whose face told that her life's holidays could without difficulty be counted; while, to a few, the fact of sitting still and looking out and feeling the quiet is pleasure enough. 'I seem to see further than ever I saw before,' murmured a pale young mother, sitting on the Upper Terrace at Hampstead, and as she said it she looked as if the sight of the country just then, when her eyes were reopened by her new motherhood, might, in another sense, make her see farther than she had ever seen before.

If the garden is small and its resources soon ended, games must be resorted to, and such games as 'tersa,' where running and motion are enjoyed ; the 'ring and the string,' when eyes and ears must be on the alert; or 'blow the candle blindfold'; all cause hearty fun, especially when the unconscious blindfold, having walked crookedly, energetically blows, as he thinks, at the candle, which is still burning steadily a yard or two from him. On some of these occasions the hostess has had her carriage out, and by taking four or five of the guests at a time all have been able to have a short drive, and see from a higher elevation something more of the country, 'Well, I don't know that I was ever in a carriage before,' said one woman, who could hardly be said to have been *in* one then, as she dismounted from the box. 'Except at funerals,' corrected her neighbour. Might not some of the extraordinary liking, which is so common among the poor, for attending funerals be partly for the sake of the rare event of a drive? Occasionally it is possible to get up a dance, with the help of a fiddle or piano, and many a pale, worn face has lost, for the time at least, its stamp of weariness as it grew interested in the ups and downs of 'Sir Roger de Coverley.' 'Bless me, if I ever thought to do any dancing, except the dancing of babbies,' was an unexpected comment from my partner on one occasion; and many times have I since been referred to to confirm the fact that 'You did see me dancing, didn't you, ma'am?'

Besides these active pleasures, there is the enjoyment of music, the love and appreciation of which is so deep and warm in these uncultured minds; music which more than anything else helps to smooth away class as well as other inequalities. I have seen rough low-class men and women leave their active games or the swing for which they had been waiting and cluster round the singer or musician begging for another and yet 'another bit.' What they like best is a song with a chorus, or historical songs where they can hear the words, and next to these solemn music on a harmonium or organ; but any music charms them, and the hostess who is either musical herself or who invites her musical friends to help her finds the task of entertaining much easier. An oft-repeated mistake is that the poor like comic songs about themselves, and 'Betsy Waring' has been suggested and sung at our parties more often than I like to remember. A moment's sympathetic thought will show, however, that the poor want other and wider interests, and it can hardly be the kindliest method of amusing them to sing them a song, the joke of which lies in imitations and 'take-offs' of their mispronunciation. It is, too, generally thought that the uneducated cannot appreciate what is commonly understood as 'good music,' but this, too, is a mistake. Long years ago I remember Mrs. Nassau Senior coming to a night-school of rough girls, held in a rough court. That evening some street row was more attractive than A B C, and our scholars were clustered around the heroine of the fight. I can still see the picture made by Mrs. Senior as she stood and sang in the doorway of the schoolroom, which opened directly on to the court, and among such surroundings it was a deep-sighted sympathy which led her to choose 'Angels ever bright and fair.' For long afterwards she was remembered as 'the lady who came and sang about the angels, and looked like one herself.'

It is well if the hostess can bring her instrument to the window, so that the people can hear as they sit on the lawn outside and enjoy the air; perhaps she may find it possible to ask two or three of her guests who can sing, with strong, sweet, though untrained voices, to join her in a duet or glee, and helping, they enjoy the pleasure with the helper's joy. Occasionally one of the party may have brought an accordion with which to aid the impromptu concert, or some one will recall the piece of poetry committed to memory long years ago, and then we have a recitation, which pleases none the less because it is 'Jim Straw's one bit,' and has been heard a few times before. If it be wet or windy the hostess may ask her guests into the drawing-room. 'You did not see the drawing-room, did you, mum?'

asked one of the guests after a party which I had been obliged to leave early; 'it was lovely, and we all sat there quite friendly-like and listened to the music. I *did* like the look of that room.' Very pregnant of influence are these introductions into a house scrupulously clean and tastily furnished—a house kept as the dwelling of every human being should be kept. Do we not know ourselves, if we go to visit a friend with a higher standard of art, morals, or culture, how subtle is the influence; how from such visits (albeit unconsciously, or at least hardly with deliberate resolve) is dated the turning towards the new light, the intention to be more perfect?

One lady, with the real feeling of hostess-ship, took her Whitechapel guests, as she would any others, into a bedroom to take their outdoor things off. Touching, if amusing, was the remark of a girl of fifteen or thereabouts who, turning to her mother, said, 'Look, mother, here's a bed with a room all to itself!' 'Has any one really slept in this white bed?' was asked by another of that same party. While to others of a rather higher class, who have been servants before marriage, the reintroduction to such a house is a great pleasure, though to them not such a revelation as it is to those who have passed all their lives in factories or workshops. It is a welcome reminder of their past, and often suggests little improvements in the arrangement of their homes. It is a means also of diffusing a love of beauty, a sense of harmony, and an artistic taste, not to be despised among those who feel that the 'Beauty of Holiness' constitutes its attraction to the right living which leads to Righteousness.

In various ways, too many to describe, but which every hostess can devise, the hours between half-past four and eight can be pleasantly filled, until the drawing in of the long summer evening brings the party to a close. The announcement of supper is generally greeted with, 'What, go home already?' or, 'The time don't go so fast working days,' but garden parties must necessarily end with daylight, and for folk up at six in the morning ten or eleven o'clock is a late enough bed hour. Supper is generally a small meal—cake, buns, or pastry, with lemonade, fruit, or cold coffee—simply a light refreshment taken standing; but some of the friends who entertain us like better to give the light meal on the arrival of the guests, and the more substantial one later. The first plan, though, is perhaps better, as the people leave their homes early, and many of them miss their dinner altogether, amid the necessary preparation for the long absence.

'Good-night, sir, and God bless you for this day!' was the farewell of one of his guests to his silver-haired host, words which struck him deeply. 'Dear me, dear me! why did I never think of it before?' he exclaimed; and really this means of doing good seems so simple and self-evident that it is to be wondered at that those working among the poor should often not know where to take their people for a day's outing. London suburbs abound with families hardly one of whom does not give a garden party in the course of the summer, and yet how few of these parties are to guests 'who cannot bid again!' The expense of such a party is certainly not the reason of its rarity. An entertainment such as I have told about, even when meat is given, does not cost more than a shilling or eighteenpence a head. The trouble cannot be the deterrent motive, for that is nothing to be compared to the trouble of a dinner-party, nor even of any ordinary 'at home.' 'The servants would not like it' is sometimes urged as a reason, but it is certainly not the experience of those who, having overcome the objections of their servants, have tried it, and found that they entered thoroughly into the spirit of a party at which they had the pleasant duty of entertaining joined to their usual one of serving, and on more than one occasion the hearty welcome given by the servants has added much to the success of our day.

Perhaps, amid the many difficulties to which modern civilisation has brought us, one of the saddest is the mutual ignorance of the lives and minds of members of the same household—an ignorance often leading to division. It may not, I think, be the least important good of these parties that they afford a subject regarding which master and servants can be, anyhow for one day, of one mind and purpose.

Neither does it require the possession of a mansion or park before such an invitation can be sent; in fact, some of the pleasantest parties have been given in the smallest gardens, where kindliness and genial welcome have made up for want of space. One lady, indeed, who was staying for the summer in lodgings in the country gave happy afternoons and pleasant memories to more than eighty people. She asked them in little groups of twelve or fourteen, took them long country rambles, or obtained permission to saunter in a neighbour's garden, and when the evenings drew in (it was in August) brought them back to her rooms, where a good tea-supper and a few songs brought the entertainment to a close.

The guests need not always be grown people. It is, perhaps, even more important to give the growing girl or the boy just entering into manhood a taste for simple pleasures. Very delightful is the interest and enjoyment of these young things in the country life and wonders. The evening sewing-class, consisting of big girls at work every day in factories; the Bible class of young men; the discussion club; the children-servants (so numerous and so joyless in our great cities)—such little groups can be found around every place of worship, or are known to every one living among or busying himself for the good of the poor. All are open to invitations, and these can be entertained even more easily than their elders. 'Don't you remember this or that?' my young friends often ask about some trivial incident long since vanished from my memory, and when, demurring, I ask 'When?' the unfailing answer, varying in form but monotonous in substance, is 'Why, that day when you took us into the country. You *can't* forget. It was grand.'

Strangely ignorant are some of these town-bred folk of things which seem to us always to have been known and never to have been taught. They call every flower a rose, and express wonder at the commonest object. 'Law! here's straw a-growing!' I once heard in a corn-field, and emerging into a fir-wood soon after, we all joined in a laugh at the remark, 'Why, here's hundreds of Christmas trees all together.' Anything, provided it is joined to active movement, without which young things never seem quite happy, serves to amuse and to pass the time. A competition to see which girls shall gather the best nosegays, the proposal to the boys to search for some animal, queer plant, or odd stone, have helped to carry the guests over many miles and through long afternoons. Perhaps one of the nicest things which any young lady can do, even if she is not able or allowed to attempt the larger undertaking of a party, is to take some ten or twelve school boys and girls for a walk on their Saturday afternoon holiday. She need keep them, perhaps, only three or four hours, when milk or lemonade and buns, got at any milk-shop, will serve as a substitute for the usual tea.

But, besides these country parties which town-dwellers are quite unable to give, there is still left to us Londoners the possibility (not to say duty) of inviting the poor to our own houses. Our poor neighbours have not been asked to many such parties, but the few to which they have been bidden have been very pleasant. At one our hostess, but lately returned from the East, had arranged *tableaux-vivants* introducing Oriental costumes in her drawing-room, and the guests were delighted at seeing the people of the one foreign nation of which they knew anything—the Bible having been the literature which made them conversant with that—as large as life, and all 'real men and solid women.' Another time a little charade was got up, and proud was the mother whose baby was pressed into early service as a play-actor. Other friends have entertained us after a visit to the Kensington Museum or Zoological Gardens, while some evenings have been passed in much the same way as by other people who meet for social pleasure; with talk, music, strange foreign things, portfolios, and puzzles, though games may, perhaps, have occupied a somewhat longer time than is usual among guests with more conversational interests. To all of us have these parties given much pleasure—pleasure which is, in truth, healthful and refreshing amid the sorrow and pain so liberally mingled in the life's cup of the poor. 'This evening I've forgot all the winter's troubles,' followed the 'Good-night' from the lips of a pain-broken woman; and considering the 'winter's troubles' included the death of a child and the semi-starvation resulting from the almost constant out-of-work condition of the husband, the party seemed a strangely inadequate means of producing even temporarily so large a result.

The efforts made to attend are one of the signs of how much these and the country parties are enjoyed. One woman came, with her puling, pink ten-days-old baby, and both men and women constantly get up from a sick-bed to return to it again as soon as the pleasure is over. 'We can't afford to lose it, yer see; they don't come too often,' is the sort of answer one usually receives in reply to remonstrance.

But this paper will accomplish its object if 'they do come oftener,' and if not only the poor of our big London, to whom we owe special duties, but if the poor of all great cities are more thought of in the light of guests.

The duty once recognised, the method becomes plain. Every one, even those whose work does not take them among the poor, can manage to be introduced to some who are leading pleasure-barren lives, and to employers of labour in factories or trades it is especially easy. The introduction made, the rest follows naturally, and though pleasure is in itself so great a good that I would hold the thing worth doing if this alone were obtained, yet I think a prophet's eye is not needed to see the other possible good resulting from such gatherings. The wider interests, the seeds of culture, the introduction to simple recreations, the suggestion of ideal beauty, the possession of happy memories, the class relationships, are the advantages one can rapidly count off as accruing to the entertained, and as important are the gains of the entertainers. The rich, coming face to face with the poor, have seen patience which puts their restlessness to shame; endurance about which poems have yet to be written; hope which is deep and springing from the roots of their being; charity which never faileth, including, as it often does, the adoption of the orphan child or the sharing of the room with a lone woman, compared to which the biggest subscription is as nothing; kindliness which, though unthinking, spareth not itself. Each class has its virtues, but, as yet, they are unknown to each other. It is for the rich to take the first step towards knowing and being known; it is for them to say if the class hatreds, which like other 'warfare comes from misunderstanding,' shall exist in our midst. It is for them to make the way of friendship through the wall of gold now dividing the rich from the poor. It is for them to give fellowship which, crushing envy, takes the sting out of poverty. And all this can be done, by spending some thought, a little money, and some afternoons in being 'At Home' to the poor.

Great ends these to follow the small trouble and expense of a garden party. It will not, though, be the first time in history that good has been done by means which seemed contemptible, and it will not seem strange to those who have learnt that it is a Life and not a law, friendships and not organisations, which have taught the world its greatest lessons.

Henrietta O. Barnett.

VI.

UNIVERSITY SETTLEMENTS.[1]

ONCE more, as happens in crises of history, rich and poor have met. 'Scientific charity,' or the system which aims at creating respectability by methods of relief, has come to the judgment, and has been found wanting. Societies which helped the poor by gifts made paupers, churches which would have saved them by preaching made hypocrites, and the outcome of scientific charity is the working man too thrifty to pet his children and too respectable to be happy.

Those who have tried hardest at planning relief and at bringing to a focus the forces of charity, those who have sacrificed themselves to stop the demoralising outrelief and restore to the people the spirit of self-reliance, will be the first to confess dissatisfaction if they are told that the earthly paradise of the majority of the people must be to belong to a club, to pay for a doctor through a provident dispensary, and to keep themselves unspotted from charity or pauperism. There is not enough in such hope to call out efforts of sacrifice, and a steady look into such an earthly paradise discloses that the life of the

[1] Reprinted, by permission, from the *Nineteenth Century* of February 1881.

thrifty is a sad life, limited both by the pressure of continuous toil and by the fear lest this pressure should cease and starvation ensue.

The poor need more than food: they need also the knowledge, the character, the happiness which are the gift of God to this age. The age has received His best gifts, but hitherto they have fallen mostly to the rich.

It is a moment of Peace. To-day there are no battles, but the returns of the dead and wounded from accidents with machinery and from diseases resulting from injurious trades show that there are countless homes in which there must still be daily uncertainty as to the father's return, and many children and wives who become orphans and widows for their country's good.

It is an age of Knowledge. But if returns were made either of the increased health due to the skill of doctors and sanitarians, or of the increased pleasures due to the greater knowledge of the thoughts and acts of other men in other times and countries, it would be shown that neither length of days nor pleasure falls to the lot of the poor. Few are the poor families where the mother will not say, 'I have buried many of mine.' Few are the homes where the talk has any subject beyond the day's doings and the morrow's fears.

It is an age of Travel, but the mass of the poor know little beyond the radius of their own homes. It is no unusual thing to find people within ten miles of a famous sight which they have never seen, and it is the usual thing to find complete ignorance of other modes of life, a thorough contempt for the foreigner and all his ways. The improved means of communication which is the boast of the age, and which has done so much to widen

H

thought, tends to the enjoyment of the rich more than of the poor.

It is an age of the Higher Life. Higher conceptions of virtue, a higher ideal of what is possible for man, are the best gift to our day, but it is received only by those who have time and power to study. 'They who want the necessaries of life want also a virtuous and an equal mind,' says the Chinese sage; and so the poor, being without those things necessary to the growth of mind and feeling, jeopardise Salvation—the possession, that is, of a life at one with the Good and the True, at one with God.

Those who care for the poor see that the best things are missed, and they are not content with the hope offered by 'scientific charity.' They see that the best things might be shared by all, and they cannot stand aside and do nothing. 'The cruellest man living,' it has been said, ' could not sit at his feast unless he sat blindfold,' and those who see must do something. They may be weary of revolutionary schemes, which turn the world upside down to produce after anarchy another unequal division; they may be weary, too, of philanthropic schemes which touch but the edge of the question. They may hear of dynamite, and they may watch the failure of an Education Act, as the prophets watched the failure of teachers without knowledge. They may criticise all that philanthropists and Governments do, but still they themselves would do something. No theory of progress, no proof that many individuals among the poor have become rich, will make them satisfied with the doctrine of *laissez faire* ; they simply face the fact that in the richest country of the world the great mass of their countrymen live without the knowledge, the character, and the fulness of life which are the best gift to this age, and that some thousands either beg for their daily bread or live in anxious misery about a wretched existence. What can they do which revolutions, which missions, and which money have not done?

It is in answer to such a question that I make the suggestion of this paper. I make it especially as a development of the idea which underlies a College Mission. These Missions are generally inaugurated by a visit to a college from some well-known clergyman working in the East End of London or in some such working-class quarter. He speaks to the undergraduates of the condition of the poor, and he rouses their sympathy. A committee is appointed, subscriptions are promised, and after some negotiations a young clergyman, a former member of the college, is appointed as a Mission curate of a district. He at once sets in motion the usual parochial machinery of district visiting, mothers' meetings, clubs, &c. He invites the assistance of those of his old mates who will help; at regular intervals he makes a report of his progress, and if all goes well he is at last able to tell how the district has become a parish.

The Mission, good as its influence may be, is not, it seems to me, an adequate expression of the idea which moved the promoters. The hope in the College when the first sympathy was roused was that all should join in good work, and the Mission is necessarily a Churchman's effort. The desire was that as University men they should themselves bear the burdens of the poor— and the Mission requires of them little more than an annual guinea subscription. The grand idea which moved the College, the idea which, like a new creative spirit, is brooding over the face of Society, and is making men conscious of their brotherhood, finds no adequate expression in the district church machinery with which, in East London, I am familiar. There is little in that machinery which helps the people to conceive of religion apart from sectarianism, or of a Church which is 'the nation bent on righteousness.' There is little, too, in the ordinary parochial mechanism which will carry to the homes of the poor a share of the best gifts now enjoyed in the University.

Imagine a man's visit to the Mission District of his college. He has thought of the needs of the poor, and of the way in which those needs are being met. He has formed in his mind a picture of a district where loving supervision has made impossible the wretchedness of 'horrible London'; he expects to find well-ordered houses, people interested in the thoughts of the day, gathering round their pastor to learn of men and of God. He finds instead an Ireland in England, people paying 3s. or 4s. a week for rooms smaller than Irish cabins, without the pure air of the Irish hill-side, and with vice which makes squalor hopeless. He finds a population dwarfed in stature, smugly content with their own existence, ignorant of their high vocation to be partners of the highest, where even the children are not joyful. He measures the force which the Mission curate is bringing to bear against all this evil. He finds a church which is used only for a few hours in the week, and which is kept up at a cost of 150*l.* a year. He finds the clergyman absorbed in holding together his congregation by means of meetings and treats, and almost broken down by the strain put upon him to keep his parochial organisation going. The clergyman is alone, his church work absorbs his power and attracts little outside help. What can he do to improve the dwellings and widen the lives of 4,000 persons? What can he do to spread knowledge and culture? What can he do to teach the religion which is more than church-going? What wonder if, when he is asked what help he needs, he answers, 'Money for my church,' 'Teachers for my Sunday school,' 'Managers for my clothing club'? What wonder, too, if the visitor, seeing such things and hearing such demands, goes away somewhat discontented, somewhat inclined to give up faith in the Mission, and, what is worse, ready to believe that there is no way by which the best can be given to the poor?

It is to members of the Universities anxious to unite in a common purpose of improving the lives of the people that I make the suggestion that University Settlements will better express their idea. College Missions have done some of the work on which they have been sent, but in their very nature their field is limited. It is in no opposition to these Missions, but rather with a view to more fully cover their idea, that I propose the new scheme. The details of the plan may be shortly stated.

The place of settlement must of course first be fixed. It will be in some such poor quarter as that of East London, where a house can be taken in which there shall be both habitable chambers and large reception-rooms. A man must be chosen to be the chief of the Settlement; he must receive a salary which, like that of the Mission curate, will be guaranteed by the College, and he must make his home in the house. He must have taken a good degree, be qualified to teach, and be endowed with the enthusiasm of humanity. Such men are not hard to find; under a wiser Church government they would be clergymen, and serve the people as the nation's ministers; but, under a Church government which in an age of reform has remained unreformed, they are kept outside, and often fret in other service. One of these, qualified by training to teach, qualified by character to organise and command, qualified by disposition to make friends with all sorts of men, would gladly accept a position in which he could both earn a livelihood and fulfil his calling. He would be the centre of the University Settlement. Men fresh from college or old University men would come to occupy the chambers as residents. Lecturers in connection with the University Extension Society would be his fellow-lecturers in the reception-rooms, and as the head of such a Settlement he would extend a welcome to all classes in his new neighbourhood.

The old Universities exercise a strange charm: the Oxford or Cambridge man is still held to possess some peculiar knowledge, and the fact that three of the most democratic boroughs are represented by University professors has its explanation. 'He speaks beautiful German, but of course those University gentlemen ought to,' was a man's reflection to me after a talk with a Cambridge professor. Those, too, who may be supposed to know what draws in an advertising poster, are always glad to print after the name of a speaker his degree and college.

Thus it would be that the head of the Settlement would find himself as closely related to his new surroundings as to his old. The same reputation, which would draw to him fellow-scholars or old pupils, would put him in a position to discover the work and thought going on around him. He would become familiar with the teachers in the elementary and middle-class schools, he would measure the work done by clergy and missionaries, he would be in touch with the details of local politics; and, what is most important of all, he would come into sympathy with the hope, the unnamed hope, which is moving in the masses.

The Settlement would be common ground for all classes. In the lecture-room the knowledge gathered at the highest sources would, night after night, be freely given. In the conversation rooms the students would exchange ideas and form friendships. At the weekly receptions of 'all sorts and conditions of men' the residents would mingle freely in the crowd.

The internal arrangements would be simple enough. The Head would undertake the domestic details and fix the price which residents would pay for board and lodging. He would admit new members and judge if the intentions of those who offered were honest. Some would come for their vacations; others occupied during the daytime would come to make the place their home. University men, barristers, Government clerks, curates, medical students, or business men each would have opportunity both for solitary and for associated life, and the expense would be various to suit their various means. The one uniting bond would be the common purpose, 'not without action to die fruitless,' but to do something to improve the condition of the people. It would be the duty of the Head to keep alive among his fellows the freshness of their purpose, 'to recall the stragglers, refresh the outworn, praise and reinspire the brave.' He would have, therefore, to judge of the powers of each to fill the places to which he could introduce them. To some he would recommend official positions, to some teaching, to some the organisation of relief, to some the visiting of the sick, and thus new life would be infused into existing churches, chapels, and institutions. Others he would introduce as members of Co-operative Societies, Friendly Societies, or Political and Social Clubs. He would so arrange that all should occupy positions in which they would become friends of his neighbours, and discover, perhaps as none have yet discovered, how to meet their needs.

In such an institution it is easy to see that development might be immeasurable. A born leader of men surrounded by a group of intelligent and earnest friends, pledged not 'to go round in an eddy of purposeless dust,' and placed face to face with the misery and apathy they know to be wrong, would of necessity discover means beyond our present vision. They would bind themselves by sympathy and service to the lives of the people; they would bring the light and strength of intelligence to bear on their government, and they would give a voice both to their needs and their wrongs. It is easy to imagine what such settlers in a great town might do, but it will be more to the point to consider how they may express the idea which underlies the College Mission—the interest, that is, of centres of education in the centres of industry, and the will of University men to acknowledge their brotherhood with the people.

If it be that the Missionary's account of his Mission district fails at last to rouse the interest of his hearers, and if his work seems to be absorbed in the effort to keep going his parochial machinery amid a host of like machines, the same cannot be the fate of the Settlement.

Some of the settlers will settle themselves for longer periods, and those who are occupied during the daytime will find it as possible to live among the poor as among the rich; but there must also be room for those who can spend only a few weeks or months in the Settlement, so that men may come, as some already have come, to East London to spend part of a vacation in serving the people. This interchange of life between the University and the Settlement will keep up between the two a living tie. Each term will bring, not a set speech about the work of the Mission, but the many chats on the wonders of human life. The condition of the English people will come to be a fact more familiar than that of the Grecian or Roman, and the history of the College Settlement will be better known than that of the boat or the eleven. On the other side, thoughts and feelings which are now often spent in vain talks at debating societies will go up to town to refresh those who are spent by labour, or to find an outlet in action.

There is no fear that the College Settlement will fail to rouse interest. Its life will be the life of the College. As long as both draw their strength from the common source, from the same body of members, the sympathy of the College will be with the people. Nor is there any fear lest the work of the settlers become stereotyped, as is often the case with the work of Missions and Societies. Each year, each term, would alter the constitution of the Settlement as other settlers brought in other characters and the results of other knowledge, or as their ideas became modified by common work with the various religious and secular organisations of the neighbourhood. The danger, indeed, would not be from uniformity of method or narrowness of aim; rather would it be the endeavour of the Head to limit the diversity which many minds would introduce, and restrain a liberality willing to see good in every form of earnestness. The variety of work which would embrace the most varied effort, and enlist its members in every movement for the common good, would keep about the Settlement the beauty of a perpetual promise.

If we go further, and ask how this plan reaches deeper than others which have gone before, the question is not so easily answered, because it is impossible to prophesy that a University Settlement will make the poor rich or give them the necessaries of true life. Inasmuch, though, as poverty –poverty in its true sense, including poverty of the knowledge of God and man – is largely due to the division of classes, a University Settlement does provide a remedy which goes deeper than that provided by popular philanthropy.

The poor man of modern days has to live in a quarter of the town where he cannot even try to live with those superior to himself. Around him are thousands educated as he has been educated, with taste and with knowledge on a level with his own. The demand for low things has created a supply of low satisfactions. Thus it is that the amusements are unrecreative, the lectures uninstructive, and the religion uninspiring. It is not possible for the inhabitant of the poor quarter to come into casual intercourse with the higher manners of life and thought except at a cost which would constitute a large percentage of his income.

I am afraid that it is long before we can expect the rich and poor again to live as neighbours: for good or evil they have been divided, and other means must, for the present, be found for making common the property of knowledge. One such means is the University Settlement. Men who have knowledge may become friends of the poor and share that knowledge and its fruits as, day by day, they meet in their common rooms for talk or for instruction, for music or for play.

The settlers will be able to join in that which is done by other societies, while they share all their best with the poor, and in the highest sense make their property common. They may be some of the best charity agents, for they will have an experience out of the reach of others, which they will have accumulated through their different agencies. As members of various secular and religious organisations, they may be able to compare notes after the day's work, and offer evidence as to how the poor live which, in days to come, might be invaluable. They may be some of the best educators, for, bringing ever-fresh stores of thought, they will see the weak spots in a routine which daily tires a child because it does so little to teach him, and they will have an opinion on national education better worth considering than the grumbles of those wearied with most things, or the congratulations of officials who judge by examinations. They may be the best Church reformers, for they will make more and more manifest how it is not institutions but righteousness which exalts a nation; how, one after another, all reforms fail because men tell lies and love themselves; and how, therefore, the first of all reforms is the reform of the Church, whose mission for the nation is that it create righteousness.

There is, then, for the settler of a University Settlement an ideal worthy of his sacrifice. He looks not to a Church buttressed by party spirit, nor to a community founded on self-helped respectability. He looks rather to a community where the best is most common, where there is no more hunger and misery, because there is no more ignorance and sin—a community in which the poor have all that gives value to wealth, in which beauty, knowledge, and righteousness are nationalised.

SAMUEL A. BARNETT.

[This paper was read at a meeting at St. John's College, Oxford, in November 1883, and resulted in the foundation of Toynbee Hall, Whitechapel, and other University Settlements in poor districts of large towns.]

VII.

PICTURES FOR THE PEOPLE.[1]

'It is folly, if nothing worse, to attempt it. What do the people want with fine art? They will neither understand nor appreciate it. Show them an oleograph of "Little Red Riding Hood," or a coloured illustration of "Daniel in the Lions' Den," and they will like it just as much as Mr. Millais's "Chill October" or Mr. Watts's "Love and Death."'

Such opinions met us at every turn when we first began to think of having an Art Exhibition in Whitechapel. But we knew that it is not only indifference which keeps the people living in the far East away from the West End Art Treasures. The expense of transit; the ignorance of ways of getting about; the shortness of daylight beyond working hours during the greater part of the year; the impression that the day when they could go is sure to be the day when the Museum is 'closed to the public'—all these little discouragements become difficulties, especially to the large number who have not yet had enough opportunities of knowing the joy which Art gives.

[1] Reprinted, by permission, from the *Cornhill Magazine*, March 1883.

'Well, I should not have believed I could have enjoyed myself so much, and yet been so quiet,' describes a lesson learnt from an hour spent in Mr. Watts's Gallery at Little Holland House; and once, after showing a party of mechanics a large photograph of the Dresden Madonna, I was asked, 'Where now can we see such things often?' while further talk on the picture elicited from another of the same group, 'But that's more the philosophy of pictures; one wants to see a great many to learn how to see them so.'

Such remarks, by no means isolated, and the proposal that we should 'get up a Loan Exhibition' from one of our active working-men friends, turned inclination into determination.

The resources at command were hardly enough to promise success in the undertaking. They were but three schoolrooms, thirty feet by sixty, behind the church, not on a central thoroughfare, and approached by a passage yard; the light was much obscured by surrounding buildings; the doorways were narrow and the staircase crooked. But friends came forward to help, and there was soon formed a large committee, which, after meeting two or three times to discuss general principles and plans, divided itself into sub-committees to carry out special branches of a work which, though to a large extent one of detail, was by no means slight.

The hanging committee undertook to measure space, obtain the sizes of pictures, and see to the strength of rods and thickness of walls, but to the general committee was left the duty of refusing undesirable-sized or inappropriate pictures. This last was by no means the least difficult labour, so extraordinary were some of the loans offered to us; a dreadful portrait of an uncomely old lady was sent because 'she was the maternal grandmother of a man who used to keep a shop in the High Street,' this recommendation being considered sufficient to obtain for the picture a place in an Art Collection; a pencil drawing 'done by John when he was only fifteen, and now he's doing well in the pawnbroking line,' was held worthy by a proud mother.

But if, on the one side, we were somewhat overwhelmed with offers of loans of doubtful description, on the other we were not unfrequently surprised at the unwillingness of art owners to lend their treasures. Vain were promises of safety and insurance. 'I don't fear for the pictures, but I don't like to have my walls bare,' was the too common answer; and the argument, 'Not for a fortnight, to enable thousands of people to see them?' rarely penetrated the coat of selfishness which incases such owners.

By no means had the hanging committee a monopoly of work. The decorative committee made it its duty to provide hangings, flags, bunting; to hide the usual schoolroom suggestions, and to make the place attractive to the passing crowd. The advertising committee undertook the difficult and expensive work of making the undertaking known, always difficult, but especially so when many of the people among whom the information has to be spread can neither read nor write. The finance committee did the dull but necessary work connected with money.

At the first Exhibition 3*d.* was charged for admission during seven days, and free admittance granted for two days. On the threepenny days 4,000 people paid or were paid for; on the free days, including Sunday, 5,000 came to see the show. The box for donations contained on the seven paying days 4*l*. 16*s*. 1*d*.; on the two free days 6*l*. 2*s*. 3*d*. The second Exhibition was opened free. In the thirteen days 26,492 people came to see it. The boxes contained 21*l*. 8*s*. 9*d*., and 4,600 catalogues were sold at 1*d*.,[1] realising 20*l*. 17*s*. 1*d*., the cost of printing of which was 17*l*. 16*s*.

Not the least weighted with responsibility was the watch committee, whose work was the safeguarding of the loans, both by night and day. Policemen, firemen, and caretakers had to be engaged, not to mention the organisation required to arrange for the eighteen or twenty gentlemen who came down daily to 'take a watch' of four hours in the rooms; where their presence not only served to prevent unseemly conduct, but their descriptions of pictures and homely chats with the people made often all the difference between an intelligent visit and a listless ten minutes' stare. The work of borrowing was everybody's work; and, on the whole, the response met with has been generous, particularly from the artists and those owners whose possessions were few.

The first Exhibition included—besides pictures—pottery, needlework, and curiosities; but, interesting as these were, the expense of getting them together, providing cases for them, and showing them thoroughly under glass, was so great that in the second Exhibition it was determined to exhibit only pictures and such works of art and curiosities as the Kensington Museum would lend

---

[1] First edition was sold at 3*d*.; and some on the first day at 6*d*., while a few were given away.

us, the latter already in cases, and with their own special caretaker to boot.

The cataloguing and describing committee comes last; and its work, though done in a hurry, bore no slight relation to the success of the undertaking.

It is impossible for the ignorant to even look at a picture with any interest unless they are acquainted with the subject; but when once the story is told to them their plain, direct method of looking at things enables them to go straight to the point, and perhaps to reach the artist's meaning more clearly than some of those art critics whose vision is obscured by thoughts of 'tone, harmony, and construction.'

Mr. Richmond's fine picture of 'Ariadne' elicited many remarks. 'Why, it is crazy Jane!' exclaimed one woman, following up the declaration in a few moments by, 'and it's finely done, too;' but the story once explained, either by catalogue or talk, the interest increased. 'Poor soul! she's seen her day,' came from a genuine sympathiser. 'Oh, no! she'll get another lover; rest sure of that.' ''Tain't quite likely, seeing that it's a desert island!' was the practical retort, which rather dumbfounded the hopeful commentator; but she would have the last word: 'Well, I would, if it were myself, and she'll find a way, sure enough, somehow.' 'The light is all behind her,' showed a delicate perception of what, perhaps, the artist himself had put in with the truth of unconsciousness.

Mr. Briton Rivière's representation of the 'Dying Gladiator' was the subject of much conversation. It is, perhaps, hardly necessary to remind any one of the picture, which was in the Academy but a year or two ago.

I

The splendid painting of the tigers, both dead and living, with the vividly depicted physical agony of the martyr, in spite of which he feels triumph, as, faithful even in death, he makes the sign of the cross in the sand, would probably make an impression on and be remembered by those who saw it.

'There, my boy, there's your ancestor in the lions' den!' was the paternal explanation of one of Abraham's descendants to his small son; but a reference to the catalogue changed his opinion on the subject, if not on the goodness of the cause for which the gladiator suffered. The description in the catalogue for this picture was: 'The Romans, for their holiday amusement, made their prisoners fight with wild beasts. The young Christian has killed one of the tigers; but is himself mortally wounded. His last act is to trace in the sand the form of a cross, the sign of the faith for which he dies. The shouts of the excited crowd, the roar of the baulked tiger, are fading in his ears. God has kissed him, and he will sleep.' Somewhat fanciful, perhaps, but reaching, maybe, the spirit of the picture more truly than a plainer statement of facts would have done. '"God kissed him," it says; I should have said the tiger clawed him,' was the one adverse criticism overheard on the description. As a rule, the subject of the picture once understood, the people stood before it in thoughtful consideration.

Mr. Richmond's 'Sleep and Death,' as well as Mr. Watts's 'Time, Death, and Judgment,' both ideal rather than historical or domestic pictures, were greatly enjoyed, and this by a class of people whose external lives are drearily barren of ideals.

PICTURES FOR THE PEOPLE

An interpretation offered by any one who had studied the parable pictures was eagerly accepted, and further thoughts suggested. 'You can't see Judgment's face for his arm,' perhaps had, perhaps had not, more meaning in it than the speaker meant; while in reference to the woman's listless dropping of her flowers from her lap in 'Time, Death, and Judgment,' the remark, 'Death does not want the flowers now she's got 'em,' told of thoughtful suffering at the apparent wastefulness of death. 'Time is young yet, then,' made one feel that the speaker had caught a glimpse of life's possibilities with which probably any number of homilies had failed to impress him.

'Sleep and Death,' depicting the strong, pale warrior borne on the shoulders of Sleep, while being gently lifted into the arms of Death—so simple in colour, pure in idea, rich in suggestion—was good for the poor to see, among whom Death is robbed of none of its terrors by the coarse familiarity with which it is treated. With them funerals are too often a time of great rowdiness, and 'a beautiful corpse' a fit spectacle for all the neighbours—even the youngest child—to be invited to see. Death treated as a tender mother-woman, hidden in the cold grey vastness surrounding her, was a bright idea, producing, perhaps, greater modesty about the great mystery. 'That's the best of the whole lot, to my mind,' came, after a long gaze, from a pale, trouble-stricken man, whose sorrows Sleep had not always helped to bear, whose loveless life had made Death's enfolding arms seem wondrous kind.

Sometimes there were discussions as to which was Sleep and which Death, ended once summarily by the loudly expressed opinion, 'It don't much matter which. I don't call it proper, *anyhow*, to see a man pickaback of an angel!'—a hypercritical sense of propriety which was hardly to be expected from the appearance of the critic.

Munkacsy's picture of the 'Lint Pickers,' lent by Mr. J. S. Forbes, aroused much interest. In the catalogue, after a short account of the artist's life and works, it was described thus: 'A soldier, with a bandaged leg, is telling the story of the war to the women and children who are picking lint to dress wounds. The different feelings with which the news is received are shown with wonderful skill in the different faces. Some are waiting to hear the worst; another has already heard it, and can only bury her face in her hands. To others it is but an interesting story; while the little child is only intent on his basket of lint.

> Man's inhumanity to man
> Makes countless thousands mourn.'

The gloom of the picture, the utter dejection of the workers, relieved nowhere by a gleam of light—even the child (around whom Hope might have hovered) finding a grim plaything in the lint—all combine to tell the tale of what the artist evidently felt—the cruelty of war. Much interest was taken in finding out, amid the darkness, the different figures in their various attitudes of active or crushed woe. It spoke, though, a little sadly for the want of joyousness in East London entertainments that more than one sightseer, *before* reading the catalogue or being helped by a verbal explanation, thought 'it was a lot of poor people at tea.'

The frames of all the pictures excited wonder, sometimes admiration not accorded to the pictures themselves; and the oft-reiterated questions, 'What, now, is it all worth? How much would it fetch?' became a little wearisome, not the less so because expressive of one of the signs of the times.

'All beautiful! and most of them [the pictures] done by machinery, I suppose,' showed greater mechanical than artistic appreciation; while the cross-examination to which we were put as to why the Exhibition was held was sometimes interesting rather than edifying. 'Oh, yes, it'll pay, sure enough, if you only go on long enough,' was one woman's comforting assurance; and the answer, 'I hardly see how, considering that it is open free,' carried so little force to her mind that its only effect was to make her repeat her belief in a still more confidently cheery tone. But many and hearty were the thanks that were given at the end of some such chats; and the gentlemen who explained the pictures and talked to the little groups which quickly gathered round 'some one who would tell about it all' were more than once offered reward-money—a flattering tribute to their powers, and illustrative of the living sense of justice in the workman's mind and the conviction that 'the labourer is worthy of his hire.'

The pathetic pictures were, perhaps, the most generally appreciated. Israel's 'Day before the Departure,' lent by Mr. J. S. Forbes, was described thus: 'The widow, utterly sad, has shut her Bible and seems heartbroken and hopeless. The child does not understand everything, but she knows her mother is sorry; the toy is forgotten, while she nestles close in her desire to comfort. Her love may be the light which will brighten the future,' often reduced the beholders to sympathetic silence; while warm was the praise given to Salentin's 'Foundling,' a pretty picture of an old yeoman giving the forsaken babe into the arms of his kindly daughters. The bright evening sky, the tender springtime, the interest of the farm-boy, and the curiosity of the sheep, all hopefully express that the little one's short, troublous day is over, and that its happier spring-time has dawned.

'Our Father's House,' by Wilfrid Lawson: the little, ragged girl peeping wistfully round the church pillar at the fashionably dressed congregation, who too often monopolise 'Our Father's House,' had always around it some quiet and earnest students. It aroused in them, perhaps, the sleeping sense, now so often forgotten that it is almost ignored, that the church is the people's possession, and, maybe, it awakened the hope, deep down (if sometimes visionary) in every breast, of the coming of the 'good time' when all class and unworthy distinctions will be lost in the Father's presence.

Israel's works, of which in the last Exhibition there were five, were duly appreciated, not perhaps by the mass, but by the more thoughtful of the spectators. 'The Canal Boat, a picture full of sadness; the man and woman look weary and worked. Nature is in tune with their hard life; still there is progress,' said the catalogue. I overheard one man say, 'Ah! poor chap, he's got into a wrong current, but he'll get out all right. Pull away.' The picture, sketchy as it was, had taught in Israel's style the lesson he loves to give—the pain

and dreariness of life interlaced with the bright thread of hope—
> Which is out of sight:
> That thread of all-sustaining beauty,
> Which runs through all and doth all unite.

Mr. Walter Crane's picture of 'Ormuzd and Ahriman,' which he kindly lent, awoke much interest. The people read, or had read to them, the description which told that the Persians believed in two gods—the god of good, Ormuzd; the god of evil, Ahriman—and how the picture expressed the fight between the two; a fight going on in every nation and every heart, all nature being represented as standing still during the conflict; while the river of time wound gently on past the ruins of the Memnons, the Acropolis, the Grove, the Altar, and the Abbey—the symbols of the world's great religions. 'I expect that's true, but we don't seem to see much of the *fight* about here,' was one cogent remark. Most frequently, though, a picture will draw forth no expression —for with the unlettered all expression is difficult, and we know how, in the presence of death, of a grand sunset, or of anything deeply moving, silence seems most fitting.

Sometimes, though, one overhears talks which reveal much. Mr. Schmalz's picture of 'Forever' had one evening been beautifully explained, the room being crowded by some of the humblest people, who received the explanation with interest, but in silence. The picture represented a dying girl to whom her lover has been playing his lute, until, dropping it, he seemed to be telling her with impassioned words that his love is stronger than death, and that, in spite of the grave and separation, he will love her *forever*. I was standing outside the Exhibition in the half-darkness, when two girls, hatless, with one shawl between them thrown round both their shoulders, came out. They might not be living the worst life: but, if not, they were low down enough to be familiar with it and to see in that only the relation between men and women. The idea of love lasting beyond this life, making eternity real, a spiritual bond between man and woman, had not occurred to them until the picture with the simple story was shown them. 'Real beautiful, ain't it all?' said one. 'Ay, fine, but that "Forever," I did take on with that,' was the answer. Could anything be more touching? What work is there nobler than that of the artist who, by his art, shows the degraded the lesson that Christ Himself lived to teach?

The landscapes were, perhaps, the pictures least cared for; and this is not to be wondered at, considering how little the poorer denizens of our large towns can know of the country, or of nature's varied and peculiar garbs, which artists delight to illustrate. 'How far is it to that place?' was eagerly asked before a picture of Venice, by R. M. Chevalier, a picture of which the description told how the Grand Canal was the 'Whitechapel Road' of Venice, and further explained the relationship of gondolas to omnibuses and cabs—a relationship not understood at once by the untravelled world. 'Would it cost much money to go and see that?' was often provoked by such pictures as Elijah Walton's picture of 'Crevasses in the Mer de Glace,' kindly lent by Mr. H. Evill, or Mr. Croft's 'Matterhorn,' lent by Mr. T. L. Devitt, and described: 'A peak in the Alps too steep for snow, and until lately too steep for mountaineers. Chains have now been placed at the most difficult places, and several English ladies have reached the top. The artist shows the loneliness of greatness :—

> The solemn peaks but to the stars are known,
> But to the stars, and to the cold lunar beams;
> Alone the sun rises, and alone
>   Spring the great streams.—MATTHEW ARNOLD.'

With the knowledge of the indifference, because of the unhelped and inevitable ignorance of the town poor in respect to landscape art, special pains were taken with the descriptions, endeavours being made to connect the landscape with some idea with which they were already familiar, or to connect it with some moral association which would attract notice to its qualities; for instance, Mr. John Brett's 'Philory, King of the Cliffs,' was brought nearer to the spectators by the suggestion that ' the coast of England was, like its people, cool and strong, and not to be hurt by a storm'; and Mr. W. Luker's picture of 'Burnham Beeches,' lent by Mr. S. Winkworth, gained in interest because the catalogue said it was 'A forest near Slough, about eighteen miles from London, bought by the City of London, and made the property of the people.'

Mr. W. S. Wyllie's 'Antwerp,' a grey, flat picture, had its idea partly embodied in 'Sea and land seemed to end in the cathedral spire'; while the familiar proverb, 'It is an ill wind that blows nobody good,' drew attention to Mr. W. C. Nakkens's 'Harvesting in Holland'; and the suggestion that 'the horses are enjoying the wind which is blowing up the rain, the farmer's enemy in harvest,' showed the standpoint from which the picture could be looked at.

Not that the catalogue was intended to contain exhaustive explanations of the pictures, but only indications of the lines along which the people could make their own discoveries. Full, however, as some of the descriptions were, they were not full enough to prevent misconceptions. A little copy of Tintoretto, lent by Mr. E. Bale, depicting the visit and embrace of the Virgin Mary and Elisabeth, simply entered in the catalogue as the 'Meeting of Mary and Elisabeth,' was mistaken for an interview between Mary, Queen of Scots, and Queen Elizabeth, and produced the reflection, 'I suppose that was before they quarrelled, then'—a sign that historical had, in this instance, made more mark than Bible instruction.

Information about Darwin, concerning whose work the catalogue was silent, was finally volunteered by one of a little group who pronounced him to be 'the Monkey Man'; and another knew no more about Gladstone than that 'he was the chap that followed Lord Beaconsfield.'

'Lesbia,' by Mr. J. Bertrand, explained as 'A Roman girl musing over the loss of her pet bird,' was commented on by, 'Sorrow for her bird, is it? I was thinking it was drink that was in her'—a grim indication of the opinion of the working classes of their 'betters'; though another remark on the same picture, 'Well, I hope she will never have a worse trouble,' showed a kindlier spirit and perhaps a sadder experience.

But the catalogue once studied, it was clung to with

almost comical persistency. A picture by Jacob Maris, lent by Mr. J. S. Forbes, of a 'Street in Amsterdam,' was next in the catalogue, though not in the room, to one of Mr. F. F. Dicksee's of 'Christ walking on the Water.' The Amsterdam picture was one in Maris's best style—a row of quaint, irregular houses, boats by the wharf, still cold water from the midst of which a post protruded, catching the light. 'No doubt a fine picture,' commented a spectator, 'but it requires a deal of imagination.' 'Why? I don't see that; it's plain enough: there are the ships, houses, wharf,' explained a friendly neighbour. 'Yes, I see all them; but it's the rest of it that wants the imagination.' Further pause, and then, 'Oh! I see; I've got the wrong number; I thought it was "Christ walking on the Water"—that's what I was looking for.'

The historical or domestic pictures, such as J. B. Burgess's 'Presentation,' the English ladies visiting the house of a Moor who is presenting his children to them; or Edwin Long's 'Question of Propriety,' the priests watching the dancing-girl to decide if the dance was proper or not, perhaps attracted the most immediate attention, just in proportion as they told their own tale; but, aided by catalogue or talk, the pictures embodying the highest spiritual truths became the most popular.

The sentiment pervading J. F. Millet's 'Angelus' which makes prayer—the communion with the 'Besetting God'—at evening time, 'Earth's natural vesper hour,' seem right and fitting was an unspoken sermon beyond their comprehension as art critics, but within their reach as men and women capable of communion with the highest. And, at present, when ordinary religious influences appear to make so sadly little impression, shall we not use such pictures also as stepping-stones towards the truer life?

Some amount of fine art is now lost to the world because the construction of most modern houses puts narrow limits to the size of pictures. 'We are often unable to express our best ideas for want of room,' I was told by a living artist whom this or any age would, I think, call great; and another painter has had what he considers his finest picture left on his hands because it is too big for any drawing-room and most galleries.

Is there not a double work here for the rich to do? Might they not, by buying such pictures, encourage the artists to paint their best thoughts, whatever size they require, thus making the world richer by enabling it to possess a little more of the knowledge gained by those who 'hang on to the sunskirts of the Most High'? Might they not put them as gifts or loans on the walls of churches or hospitals, making bare walls speak great truths, not the less audible because of the murmur of the people's thanks, real, if unheard by the donors?

Pictures will not do everything. They will not save souls, for 'it takes a life to save a life'; but shall such works be kept only for the amusement or passing interest of the rich? Shall not we, who care that the people should have life and fuller life, press them into the service of teaching? Words, mere words, fall flat on the ears of those whose imaginations are withered and dead; but art, in itself beautiful, in ideas rich, they cannot choose but understand, if it be brought within their reach.

Art may do much to keep alive a nation's fading

higher life when other influences fail adequately to nourish it; and how shall we neglect it in these hard times of spiritual starvation? In Mrs. Browning's words

'The artist keeps up open roads between the seen and the unseen. Art is the witness of what *is* behind the show.'

HENRIETTA O. BARNETT.

VIII.

THE YOUNG WOMEN IN OUR WORK-HOUSES.[1]

Those of us who have ever entered a workhouse will not easily forget some of the sad impressions then made upon the mind. We remember the large, dreary wards—

> The walls so blank,
> That my shadow I thank
> For sometimes falling there—

the cleanliness which is oppressive, the order which tells of control in every detail. But, gloomy as these things are, they are but the necessary surroundings of many of the people who come to end their days amid them. On their faces is written failure; having been proved useless to the world, they are cast away out of sight, and too often out of mind, on to this sad rubbish-heap of humanity.

A closer inspection of this rubbish-heap, however, shows that it is not all worthless. Besides the many whom dissolute, improvident, or vicious courses bring to the workhouse, there are some who are more sinned against than sinful; some who are merely unfortunate,

[1] Reprinted, by permission, from *Macmillan's Magazine*, August 1879.

and who by a little wise help, wisely given, may become useful members of society.

It is of the young, single women that I would specially speak. Those whom one finds in the workhouse are usually there for one of three reasons. First, in order to seek shelter when about to become mothers; secondly, because they are driven thither by the evil results of profligacy; thirdly, because having failed in life they choose to enter there rather than to sin or to starve. It is of the first and third classes that I now write, for the second class is being dealt with, if not efficiently, at least earnestly, by many societies founded for that purpose.

From June 1877 to June 1878 in the seven unions of East London alone there have been no less than 253 young girl-mothers who have entered the infirmaries.

Some enter a few months before their confinement, driven to that inhospitable shelter from the sense of the value of their remaining character. And here a word is required as to the neglect of any proper method of classification. There should be in all our workhouses accommodation which would allow of the separation of characters among classes; and power and encouragement should be given to the master and matron to carry this plan into effectual working. The more respectable of the young women might be placed under the supervision of one of the staff, so that the time which necessarily elapses before they can be again sent out should be to them a time of instruction in what is good and desirable, instead of, as it now too often is, a time when they are corrupted by the evil influence of others worse than themselves.

But these 253—what becomes of them? On their

recovery they cannot remain in the infirmary, and must be sent to the able-bodied house, there to live on prison fare and to associate with the criminal and wilfully idle. Rather than do this many a young woman prefers to go out, taking her three-weeks-old babe with her, resolved to 'get on' as best she can. That 'best' is often the 'worst.' With her character gone, with two mouths to feed instead of one, and with the loss of self-respect rapidly following the loss of the respect of others, the unfortunate mother too often falls into hopeless vice; or, perhaps, the giant temptation presents itself of sacrificing the little wailing life which stands between her and respectability. Unhelped, unencouraged as they are, who can wonder that such mothers, so sorely tried, sometimes fall, and that the crime of infanticide is horribly rife?

But, frequent as such results are, the end is not always thus tragic; the ruined girl often returns to her father's house and to the same conditions of life as before she fell. But this course, though not so apparently bad, is yet often very harmful. Her presence familiarises the younger members with vice, an unadvisable familiarity; for vice, while it gains much attractive power, gains also more deterrent force by its mystery in the minds of the young.

Sometimes the unwedded mother, on leaving the workhouse, honestly tries to get work at sack-making, factory-work, anything which will enable her to keep her little one near her; but it is a hard, an almost impossible task. The care of the child impedes the work, and thus it has to be put out to daily nurse. The ignorance, if not the apathy, of its badly paid nurse and the unsuitability of its food too often combine to extinguish the little flame which was burning to guide its mother back to virtue by the paths of love and self-control.

These, briefly, are some of the present evils which beset the lives of the young women who become mothers in our workhouses.

It was to cure some of such evils that a few ladies associated themselves together in the spring of 1876. We bound ourselves by no rules or bye-laws, for the work is one which is entirely of an individual nature. Strong personal influence has to be brought to bear on each applicant, with a distinct and definite object in view, suggested by the character of the woman and the circumstances of the case. There have been, unfortunately, changes in our workers, but we have continued to visit, with fair regularity, both the infirmary and able-bodied house of our Union. When work is necessarily left so largely to individual initiative, depending on the character of the worker, each lady must, naturally, adopt her own method of doing it. Some feel that they can do more *for* the girls by changing the circumstances of their lives, while others can do more *with* them by arousing their dormant moral natures and filling them with enthusiasm for good. But all ways of doing the work are needed, the more diverse the means the larger the number of women likely to be reached. The very diversity of the means makes it difficult, however, to write about the work as it is done by all the co-operators. It is, therefore, well that I should speak only of my own plan and experiences.

I visit about once a week, and see alone in a room, which the matron kindly lends for the purpose, each girl who has expressed a wish to lead a good life. After talking to her and learning of her antecedents, her statements are sent to the Charity Organisation Society to be verified. I try to learn something of her character, of the ideal she has of her own life, of the plans she has made for the future, of the kind and manner of good which appears to her most attractive and desirable. On receipt of the Report of the Charity Organisation Society each girl is dealt with in accordance with her past life; she who has suffered from the allurements and excitements of the town is sent into the country, being placed where the monotony and peace will protect her from herself; she who has for long lived a lawless and undisciplined life is induced to enter a Home or Refuge, where order and control will teach her the unlearnt lessons; while sometimes it is possible to get for her for whom drink has been too strong a situation with a teetotal family, who will help her by example as well as principle. For the woman whose maternal feeling wants frequent contact with her child to invigorate it a place is got where the mistress, knowing all the facts, will allow her servant often to see the little one; while the mother, whose sense of shame is stronger than her love for the child, is sent to a place far removed from the caretaker of her baby, trusting that the money which she weekly sends for it will keep in remembrance the sin of which she has been guilty and the innocent result of it.

It is a common idea that the only way of helping women sunk so low as these is to send them to Homes. This idea I would like to modify. Homes are very valuable in giving girls the opportunities of re-earning a character when, as they themselves say, they have 'no one to speak for them.' Still, in all these cases where the fault which brought them to the workhouse (serious as it may be) has not undermined the whole character, it is, perhaps, better to send them at once to service. In their mistresses' houses they are, unconsciously, guarded from the grosser temptations which lone girls have to meet, being guided by influence rather than rule. The regular, if at times too hard, work of service demanded by the varying interests and needs of a family is the greatest help to a healthy tone of mind. In a good home they see family life in all its beauty, they see the commonplace virtues in a beautiful and attractive setting, and the kindliness which is engendered between the served and the server helps the poor stumbling soul along the path of duty over many a rough and difficult place. 'Oh! ma'am,' a girl said the other day, 'the missus's baby is such a dear; he do make me forget such a lot;' a forgetfulness which was in her case the first necessary step towards a fairer future.

It is a good rule to tell every circumstance, however trivial, to the mistress, so that she can become in her turn the guardian of her servant against the besetting sin; and all honour be to those many ladies who have so generously come forward to take these girls into their own homes, sometimes giving them more wages than their services warranted, often helping them with clothes both for themselves and their children, and giving them too that priceless sympathy which outweighs every other gift. Such help saves more pain and makes more righteousness than big, barren subscriptions to far-off institutions; for

> The gift without the giver is bare.

If the girl has been a servant before, she can obtain 15*l*. or 16*l*. a year; out of this she can pay 4*s*. or 4*s*. 6*d*. a week, and her lady friend can assist her by paying 1*s*. or 6*d*. a week towards her baby's support. If the girl has never been a servant, it is necessary that she should enter service at a much lower wage. She must then get more money assistance, the sum being decided by the rough estimate that she should pay two-thirds of her money, whatever it is.

The small payment has many advantages; it enables the mother to disassociate herself from her past corrupting association; it assists her lady friend to keep up constant communication with her, whereby she is enabled to advise about her future, her change of place, her friends; and it also enables a watchful eye to be kept on the little one. Its nurse coming weekly to receive the money can tell of its progress, the lady can see if it is well cared for, and can by her interest encourage the nurse to do her best. As a rule the caretakers become very fond of their little charges. In one instance the mother having, alas! again returned to evil ways, the nurse continued to keep the baby without payment, jealously guarding him against his mother, 'who might harm him when in drink.' Another woman came to ask for a nurse-child because, she said, she had had fourteen children of her own, and now that they were all out in the world, 'her old man said it was so lonesome-like.' It is important, too, to choose the nurse carefully, for she has frequently a great influence on the mother, who will naturally be more inclined to listen to the wise words of one who is 'good to her baby' than to any mere well-wisher. The mother by this means gains a respectable friend of her own class, in many cases the first she has ever known. In one instance the nurse did what others had failed to do. The mother was one of those people to whom pleasure is as necessary as food and air. Among happier surroundings her sense of fun and capacity for enjoyment would have been a source of brightness, and rendered her a general favourite. For those in her sphere of life joy is an element considered unnecessary, and thus is a dangerous luxury. She had no desire to do wrong nor to offend, but pleasure she must have, and not being able to obtain it innocently, she took it lawlessly. Such conduct mistresses rightly would not allow, and she reached the workhouse when her boy was about three years old. There seemed to be no trace of affection for the child, nor any feeling beyond a sense of irritation at its helplessness and a desire to get it 'into a home,' and to be rid of the attendant responsibility. This last idea it was impossible to entertain, for responsibility might become her schoolmaster, and lead her up 'the difficult blue heights.'

She was a thorough general servant; hence there was little difficulty in getting her into a place. A home for the boy was found, with a most demonstrative and affectionate nurse, who rarely spoke of him except as a 'pretty lamb,' and who loudly and frequently called on all to admire him. Little by little this influenced the young mother, who began to be interested in the much-talked-of and cared-for baby. The deducted wages were more cheerfully rendered for its support, and as love obtained admittance to her heart, and all the many cares which accompanied a child brought interest into her life, there became less need for the outside pleasures. The craving for enjoyment found satisfaction in giving joys to the baby boy.

It would be easy to give many instances of the success of this work, but one or two will suffice. Jane, a motherless girl of sixteen, brought up in a rough, low-class home, and sent to earn her bread before she could well distinguish good from evil—what wonder that she came into the only asylum open to her, harmed by the first man who had ever shown her a kindness? She appeared indifferent to her fate, but she showed such passionate and self-giving devotion to the child that it seemed possible that the mother's character would be awakened by her feelings. They were accordingly placed in a house where they could be together; the child soon died, and Jane having greatly improved, she was sent to a situation, where she is doing well, and has got again some of the brightness of youth.

Emma, a woman of twenty-six, had for some years lived abroad with a man who promised her 'English marriage,' but who, on reaching England, basely deserted her. Characterless and unknown as she was, she tried in vain to get work to support herself and child; and at last, half dead with privation, she entered the 'House.' She had not a reference to give, nor a friend to apply to, but she did so thoroughly and well the work which the Matron gave her, and so earnestly pleaded to have a trial, that, trusting in my opinion of her sincerity, a good woman in the country took her as servant, who now, after two years of trial, writes to ask that other servants may be sent to her 'as good as Emma.' Her boy is placed in a village a few miles off, and all the holidays, most of the money, and many of the spare moments are given to him, in whom is treasured the one bright memory of her dreary past.

But of each girl that is helped such pleasant stories cannot be told. There are many failures: women whose resolution deserts them before the old temptations, whose promises are as lightly broken as they were earnestly made; girls whose ill companions offer them bright if lawless lives, and who leave the new hard ways for the well-known aimless, careless life.

But, in spite of many failures, the work is hopefully continued in the belief, founded on experience, that the idle can be induced to work and learn through daily labour the gospel which work teaches; that the coarse-minded can yet see the beauty of holiness if it is shown greatly and plainly; that the ignorant can yet be taught if patience be given; that the careless may yet be circumspect if cared for. Failures and disappointments are inevitable when the aim is not to make a temporary improvement, but to raise the ideas and radically change the habits of a class, to help whom there has hitherto been so little effort made.

But there is yet the third class of girls who have been cast by the wave of misfortune into the workhouse. These are not touched by the societies for befriending young servants, for many have never been servants, and some have started on their career before the societies were formed. Some come in because their parents break up their homes and altogether 'enter the House.' In such a plight was poor Martha, a sickly girl of eighteen, too crippled to be fit for manual work. Her father was dead; her mother was so drunken that the workhouse was for her the only resort; and thither she came bringing her children with her, and among them the poor weak Martha. The other children were sent to the district schools, but the cripple was too old to go there. There was nothing for her but to drag on a loveless, cheerless life and make her home in that unhomely place. She was a bright willing lassie, but her labour, such as it was, was not needed there, where she was but one of the many useless ones who help to give trouble and swell the rates. She was deft with her fingers and capable, if not of entirely supporting herself, still of adding wealth to the world by her work. A home was soon found for her where she could be taught straw-basket work, and on drawing the attention of the Guardians to her case, they at once consented to pay for the training. We occasionally see her. She has been taught to read and write, and to make bonnets and baskets quickly and well. She is very happy, and, though sighing when speaking of the workhouse, she adds in the same breath, ' The Matron was real good to me there.'

Some seek the workhouse because, having lost their places and being alone in the world, they know not where else to go. Some having drifted there more than once arouse the contempt and antagonism of the officers; and these, unloving and indifferent because unloved, lose all hope and interest, and grow stubborn and hard. To these girls the lady must show herself their friend, and awaken their interest in life. One girl was sent to me, not yet twenty-one, who had passed through innumerable situations, who had been for six years in and out of the House continually, and who had once been sent to prison for a breach of the necessary discipline. She was pronounced ' incorrigible ' by the authorities. I confess to having felt powerless to work her reformation when I saw her. Her stubborn set face, her downcast dull eyes, her stolid refusal to speak in reply to whatever was said, her apathy on all subjects made me feel that I had not a chance of touching her. I tried all ways, but at last aroused her by asking her to do something for me. The God-born sense of helpfulness in her awoke her sleeping soul. She felt she cared for the one person in all the world whom she had ever helped, and that affection has been her 'saving grace.' She is now earning 12*l.* a year, more, as she says, than she had 'earned in two years afore,' and her face, manners, and character are rapidly improving. She comes to me to help her to choose her new clothes, and I could not but be satisfactorily amused when the 'incorrigible' pauper insisted on having a 'high art' coloured dress, declaring that none of the others suggested were 'half so pretty.' Many such stories could be told, many beginning brightly and ending sadly, some turning out better than their commencement would have justified us in hoping. One poor child, motherless and worse than fatherless, after a short training in a Home, is now in service, and paying towards the support of her younger sister; another has a conscience so awakened as to make her hesitate for long as to her right to be confirmed because of the sin ignorantly committed which brought her to the rates, while tales could be told of women, rough and untutored, who have joyfully taken the hard, self-restraining path which leads to righteousness, and who, having once been given great ideals, receive them as new truths, and patiently (pathetically so among their rude surroundings) endeavour to live up to them.

Enough may have been said to induce other ladies to adopt the work. Taking the figures of the last two years' work at one workhouse, we have seen 141 women. Of these we have sent out, to service or to work, ninety-five; and out of these only five have again returned to the workhouse. Of many we have lost sight, which is not to be wondered at when the ignorance of the women of this class is considered. A letter is to them a thing to be much pondered, but rarely attempted. Some, after long silences, reappear to ask advice in some temporary difficulty or to tell of progress made. Many remain close friends, coming to call on every holiday or writing long and affectionate letters. One wrote the other day a stilted letter of thanks 'for having altered her position in the world for one of more sterling worth.' Her future did look gloomy when first we became acquainted. She was the daughter of a seaside lodging-house keeper, brought up in a cheap (and nasty!) boarding-school, and sent to London, with many false ideas about work, and some true ones about wickedness, to earn her living in any 'genteel' employment. Her superficial education did not help her, and she came down lower and lower, till at last, finding herself in a lodging-house of doubtful reputation, she rightly chose the workhouse in preference to remaining there. Her widowed mother, unable to keep her, and fearful that her frivolities would influence badly her younger sisters, refused to receive her home. Her fine-ladyism and ignorance of any sort of household work were an effectual barrier to her taking service, while her sorry education prevented her even trying to teach. Service seemed to be the best opening for her, and the life best calculated to keep her straight. With some difficulty she was persuaded to look at it in this light, and then induced to enter a servants' training home. She has earned good testimonials there, and is now a happy and useful servant.

The work is in itself simple, and yet has issues important, not only to the individuals helped, but to the community at large, for it tends to lessen pauperism, prostitution, and infanticide. It would be well if every lady of England were to consider how she can take part in it. If she is not herself able to visit the workhouse, she can, perhaps, open her house and heart to one of these girls who so sadly need such protection and care. Or, if that be impossible, she might undertake to befriend one of them.

Around every workhouse a committee of ladies might be formed. The meetings need not, perhaps, be formal nor frequent, but merely friendly gatherings to compare experience and to discuss reports of the work done. The visiting of the workhouse is, perhaps, for reasons which will be appreciated by those who are familiar with official establishment, better left to two or three of the members who, after seeing the girls and learning their histories, should pass one or more to each member of the committee to provide for. Every lady might be a member of such a committee. Every woman can befriend another, and perhaps may be the more moved to do so when she who needs the help is a girl no older than her own daughter in the schoolroom. There are few who cannot help the work of such committees by contributing 1s. a week for the helping of one little baby. Every one can spare a little of that loving care, can give a little of that all-saving friendship which so lavishly surrounds the life of most of us.

The work, too, is one which married ladies with homes, families, and social duties can easily take up. Women in this position are debarred from much work for the poor, because their natural and more sacred duties forbid them to run risks of infection or to take up work which would necessitate the devoting of a regular fixed day. But from both these disadvantages the work now under consideration is quite free. In the workhouse the visitor is safe from infection; the visits can be made at any time, for the women are always there, and there is always somebody waiting to be helped whenever one can go. It is, of course, better to fix a regular day for visiting if possible, so that those girls who have been seen once should be able to anticipate the second visit; but this is not at all essential, and frequently the duties of a mother or mistress do not permit of long absences from home. This work, excepting the periodical visit to the workhouse, can be done almost entirely from the writing-table in one's own house. It necessitates a good deal of correspondence in order to insure obtaining suitable situations and respectable nurses; but it requires comparatively little absence from home, for when the girl is once placed, the friendly connection can best be established and kept up in the lady's own house. There she can receive her otherwise friendless visitor; there she can strengthen the gentle bonds already begun in the House; there she can show to the homeless one some of the possibilities of home, and by such simple natural acts sow seed which will bring forth much good and happiness.

It is entirely a homely and personal work done in the

home and in the interests of the individual and of the family; one full of elements of difficulty and frequently of disappointment and failure. It requires no costly machinery: wherever there is one woman who cares for other women; wherever there is a home full of the joys of family life; wherever two or three can meet together in common work, there is all the force that is required. If in every union and all its parishes, or even in many unions and some of their parishes, those who think that the work which has been done by a few working together is a useful one will take up their part of the burden as it lies near their door, the work may grow. If it grow naturally and by no enforced development, its results may be larger than can yet be foreseen. New thought may develop new plans, wider interest may bring wider change. Our workhouses may become the means of restoring to joy and self-respect many who now leave their walls sad and degraded. Society may be strengthened by the new link between the envied rich and the unknown pauper, a link of unassailable strength being formed of love and service. And if none of these things come to pass, the effort must still be good which rouses into action a part of that family life which in its rest is so beautiful.

HENRIETTA O. BARNETT.

IX.

A PEOPLE'S CHURCH.[1]

'THE object of the British Constitution is to get twelve honest men into a jury box,' is an old-fashioned saying, which puts shortly enough the far-off end of our laws and institutions. The jury box may not itself survive, but whatever takes its place must in the same way depend on an honest public opinion. The object of the British Constitution is to secure freedom for thought and honesty among men. When its laws are enforced by the service of the citizens, and when the citizens are honest, politicians may cease to think of the need of a reform.

Reforms in the Constitution are now urged because they will make possibilities for greater honesty and greater devotion, but if the possibilities are not used the reforms will make little change for the better. A man who has a vote may be put within reach of a higher virtue, but if he gives his vote dishonestly the reform which enfranchised him will not tend to progress. A tenant who is secured from eviction, and the landlord out of whose hands the power to evict has been taken,

[1] Reprinted, by permission, from the *Contemporary Review* of November 1881.

may thank the land-law reformers, who have made honesty more easy; but if the tenant uses his power to make slaves of his labourers or his children, and the landlord his freedom from responsibility to do what he likes, the last state will be little better than the first. A population which is educated, through the efforts of the educational reformers, may have new capacities for virtue; but if they who are educated use their powers only to take care of themselves, there may at last be a difficulty in getting any to serve as jurymen.

The self-devotion which makes men willingly leave business to do some public duty, and the honesty which makes them subject interest to justice, are essential to the greatness and happiness of the people.

No Constitution can, therefore, neglect the means which are to develop these qualities. Neglect of duty is punished by fines, performance of duty is rewarded by the honours of title; dishonesty is prevented by a system of checks, which is ever being elaborated by new laws. All such means fail, and it has become a proverb that virtue cannot be made by Act of Parliament.

The Church is a part of the British Constitution, and is the means by which in old days honesty was promoted; and if in these modern days the Church fails, its failure, at any rate, has given no ground for a corresponding proverb, that virtue cannot be made by a religious agency. The majority still believe that if men were spiritually-minded they would care for things that are honest, and give themselves to duty in the spirit of the saints and puritans. There may be a morality which is independent of religion; but there is still confidence in the power of the Spirit to carry men over the rough road of duty. There is still a willingness to trust in spiritual agencies to promote morality.

Stated widely, the Church exists to spiritualise life. The ritual and the doctrine, which are often regarded as ends, are the means to this further end. A National Church exists to connect the life of individuals and the life of the nation with the life of God, in Whom all fulness is, to fill men with grace and truth, to make them to respond to high emotions and settle them on eternal calm. Its object is to make men friends, to unite all classes in common aims, to give them open minds, willing to learn, and to introduce them to whatever is honest and of good report. The Church aims to develop the sense of duty through the sense of God.

That the Church of England should fail to reach this object is not surprising. In an age of free trade, as a 'protected' society, it starts at a disadvantage. In an age of self-government, as a system which is not under popular control, it is suspected. In a democratic age, as an aristocratic organisation, it is not understood.

Chivalry worked well in its own day. The times changed, and there was no room in the new age for knights errant. Many were sorry to see it pass away, with its swift remedies for wrong, its attractive dress, and its power for good. They tried to revive its force, and 'Don Quixote' is a satire on the effort. The good man, with all his devotion, was out of place; the knight of the old age was the butt of the new age. Such a satire might be made on a Church which tries by old forms and through an old constitution to spiritualise life. A few followers may be attracted by sentiment, clinging to memories of good old times, and by striking forms of devotion; but the many will be bound to feel that the effort with all its beauty is out of place, that the realities of the old age have become the pictures of the new age.

The Church of England is not therefore effective to spiritualise the life of the nation and to develop honesty of living. Its present position is indeed indefensible. As a 'Reformed' Church, it offers the example of the greatest abuses. As a 'Catholic' Church, it promotes the principle of schism. As a 'National' Church, it is out of touch with the nation.

There is no other department in the State which can match the abuses connected with the sale of livings, with the common talk about 'preferment' and 'promotion,' with the irremovability of indolent, incapable, and unworthy incumbents, with the restriction of worship to words which expressed the wants of another age, and with the use of tests to exclude from the ranks of ministers those called by God to teach in fresh forms the newest revelations to mankind. There are no greater supporters of the schism from which they pray to be delivered than the bishops and clergymen who talk of 'the Church' as if it were a sect to promote 'Church of England' societies, and strive to cut off from the body of the people a section of its members. There is nothing national which so little concerns the nation as its Church. By the vast majority of those who are the coming rulers, namely, by the working class, the Church and its services are unused. The parson may here and there be popular as a man; he may even be regarded as

L

of some use to take the chair at meetings to get up charitable societies and promote the education or the amusement of the people. He is not, though, looked to for the help he can give to life, and it is not through him that the people hope to get vice put down, virtue promoted, and life spiritualised.

The place of the Church in the Constitution is forgotten; so when there is a complaint that impurity is sapping the strength of the nation, or that cheating is ruining trade, or that selfishness is making men scamp work, it is not the clergy who are called on to do their duty and make a cure, but a new society is formed or a new law is demanded, and the clergy are not even rebuked for neglect. No one seems to expect that a Church, nominally co-extensive with the nation, which is established to spiritualise life, should do its work. The position is indefensible. Those politicians who are moved only by agitation may say, 'The condition of the Church is not one of practical politics,' and pass on. The greater number realising that the ultimate conflict is between those who would govern with God and those who would govern without God, and anxious that the Church should be effective for its purpose, are quietly making up their minds to one of two solutions—Disestablishment or Reform.

The present means for making the people virtuous or honest fail. 'Disestablish,' urge the Liberationists. 'Let the clergy of the Church be stirred by competition and roused by interest, and we shall have better results.' 'Let the connection with the State continue,' say the Reformers; 'let the abuses be eradicated, but leave the teachers of the nation to be moved by duty and not by

bigotry or sectarian rivalry.' These two solutions for
making effective the means of developing honesty offer
themselves for examination. It is worthy of remark that
the common arguments for Disestablishment, except
those urged by the opponents of all religion, hardly touch
the principle of Establishment. Secularists urge that
religion being useless and spirituality a fancy, it is no
business of the State to do anything to spiritualise the
life of its members as a means to increase virtue. Their
position is unassailable, and the day on which the nation
decides that God has no relation to life, the Church as a
spiritualising agency must be disestablished, its buildings
turned into lecture-halls, and its endowments devoted to
the reduction of the national debt or to the teaching of
art and science.

The position of the Secularists is occupied by few.
The ordinary advocate of Disestablishment is anxious
that the life of the nation may be spiritualised, but he
sees that the Church is ineffective, he marks its abuses,
its rivalry with the sects, and its assumption of superiority. He argues that its ineffectiveness and its
assumption are due to its connection with the State, and
urges that Disestablishment alone will sweep out the
abuses. He condemns abuses but he cannot condemn a
principle which affirms the duty of the State to teach the
higher life, because he himself has probably approved the
principle as a supporter of Education Acts, liquor laws,
and other legislation of a like aim.

It is allowed by the majority of the people that
the State should teach the life of prudence, and schools
are established under local School Boards to teach every
child, so that he may earn his living. Further, it is

allowed that the State should control the forces which, for good or evil, may rouse the people, and thus licensing boards are established to limit the sale of strong drink.

The same principle is involved in an Established Church. If the State educates the citizens, and admits its responsibility for the formation of their characters, a line can hardly be drawn at a point which would exclude it from giving the people the means which are the best security for happiness and for morality.

The principle of Establishment does not — as its opponents often think—assert that a sect has truth; it asserts that the nation has truth, or is seeking it. The truth abides in the best thought of the whole nation, and the Church is established to express that truth. The clergy have no special rights, they are servants appointed to do the will of the nation. Truth abides not in 'the Church' of the bishops and clergy nor in a book, it abides in the people. Once when it was proposed in the House of Commons to refer a matter of doctrine to the bishops, 'No, by the faith I bear to God,' said Mr. Wentworth, with the approval of the House, 'we will pass nothing before we understand what it is, for that were to make you Popes.' It is the people, therefore, which by its Parliament has settled, and may again settle, the limits of teaching and ritual. The clergy are its servants paid out of funds set apart for this special purpose. Lord Palmerston put it shortly when he said, 'The property of the Church belongs to the State.'

The nation, in old language, is holy. The body of people called English is set apart for a special service, its laws are laws of God, its work is worship, and every one of its members owes a duty to God. The memory of such a fact was kept alive in Israel where every town's meeting was a congregation, every parliament a solemn assembly, every law the Word of God, and every workman was inspired by the Spirit of God. The Jewish nation has been preserved in the Jewish Church. That the English nation is holy must also be kept alive. The nation, that is, must be a Church and its citizens organised for worship. 'The spirit of nationality,' says Burke, 'is at once the bond and the safeguard of nations; it is something above laws and beyond thrones, the impalpable element, the inner life of states.' In his own language Burke asserts the holiness of nations, and it is to protect this impalpable element that it becomes so important for nations to identify their secular and religious aspects, to be at once nations and churches with duties to men and to God.

Disestablishment denies this holiness, and so lets escape the strongest element in nationality. Disestablishment is, moreover, a short-sighted policy, because, however great be the measure of Disendowment, it would make the Church of England the strongest of the sects. In a short time one of the parties now held in union within the Establishment would obtain the supremacy, and that party would inherit all the power and prestige of the position. This party—being only a section of the religious body—would pose as the representative of religion, and its clergy would identify their interests with the interest of God. Again, there would be some Becket to oppose the will of Parliament, and to call some law affecting his order 'irreligious,' and a clericalism would be let loose to assume, and perhaps make hateful, the name of religion. 'Clericalism is the enemy of men,' is a saying which has much truth in it. The pity is if clericalism and religion are enabled to seem to be the same thing.

Disestablishment, finally, would intensify the competition of sects. To make one proselyte, the supporters of various forms would compass sea and land. The standard of morality would be lowered and the flags of doctrine, invented out of will-worship, would be waved to bring in rich adherents, and get the use of their money. Even, as it is, there is no need to go far to find work, which would fall to pieces if the preacher spoke the truth to the subscribers about their private life or their tempers. It is urged that the congregations in American non-established Churches are large; it is not urged that the people in America are above bribery in politics or above cheating in trade. It is not urged that American social life is spiritualised, and that is the only fact which would be evidence of the good of the system.

To sum up the case against those who offer Disestablishment of the Church as an answer to the question, 'How is the nation to be brought into union with the spirit of goodness?' it may be urged that—

1. Disestablishment is a destructive and wasteful method of getting rid of abuses, and would destroy the power of the State to teach what the State holds to be truth.

2. Disestablishment would establish clericalism, a force which more than once in history has made religion hateful, and roused for its repression the God-fearing men of the nation.

3. Disestablishment, trusting to competition, would leave poor neighbourhoods unhelped. A poor congre-

gation could not hope for a church in which worship should be stirred by the beauty of sight and sound. An ignorant population would not exert itself to get either a church or a teacher. The most needy would thus be the most neglected. It is only the State which can give with equal hand to all its members, and which thus can either educate or spiritualise the masses.

The solution offered by those who say, 'Reform the Church,' remains for examination.

These, like the religious liberationists, are anxious that the instrument for spiritualising life should be effective. The Reformers, though, recognise that this, the highest object of any organisation is also the object of the State, and can only be attained by means of the Constitution. Individuals may be left to provide for the wants they have recognised. The State must provide for the wants of the higher life and send out teachers to tell individuals of things beyond their ken. The Church reformers urge, therefore, that the principle of Establishment should be retained, but that abuses should be eradicated and old-fashioned methods reformed.

The practical difficulties of reform are doubtless many, but they are not insuperable. Inasmuch as Burke has said, 'What is taught by a State Church must be decided by the State, and not by the clergy,' it is possible to conceive that the nation, and not a sect, might determine how truth should be sought and taught. Inasmuch as now it is the people who directly or indirectly appoint their rulers, it is easy to conceive how the people, and not a patron, might have a voice in the choice of the parson, and how the parishioners, and not the parson, might govern the Church and the parish. There need be no ill-paid, no over-paid, no unworthy incumbent. There need be no neglected parish, and a State Church might be as effective an organisation for promoting spirituality as the State Post-office is for promoting intercourse.

Institutions have survived a greater reform than that which is required in the Church, and those who have seen the changes which the law-making department of the State has endured may without fear submit the right-making department to like changes.

It is no new principle to reform the Reformed Church. By a law of Henry VIII. the king has authority to 'reform, correct all errors, heresies and abuses,' and the people's Parliament now takes the place of the king. 'The particular form of Divine worship,' says the preface to Edward VI.'s second Prayer Book, 'and the rites and ceremonies appointed to be used therein, being in their own nature indifferent and *alterable*, and so acknowledged, it is but reasonable, &c. &c.' The Long Parliament changed the whole Constitution and Ritual of the Church. The Restoration Parliament undid that work. Throughout the seventeenth century the Teaching, the Ritual, and the Organisation were discussed as open questions, and the present system is the result purely of a Parliamentary decision.

Three hundred years ago, to suit the new age, the new birth of learning, the Church was reformed. The present times are marked by changes as great as those of the Renaissance, and the Church remains unchanged. As was the Church of the sixteenth century, so is the Church of the nineteenth century.

The government of England has become popular,

and the people elect the Parliament which makes the laws; the Church of England is still exclusive, and the clergy in 'their' churches and 'their' parishes are still supreme.

Freedom has destroyed monopolies; and, according to a rough scale, justice is equally administered. In the Church, monopolies still exist, justice is defied in arrangements which are for the benefit of the strong, and the clergy are a 'protected' class.

The language and the fashion of Englishmen have changed, but the Church still addresses men with the language and the ritual of the Middle Ages.

The Church, once reformed to suit new needs, the rites of which are 'alterable,' has not been made to suit the needs of modern times. The Church must be again reformed. If details be asked as to the Constitution of the Church of the future, if questions rise to men's lips, 'What will be done about Bishops?' 'Who will fix the limits of doctrine?' 'How will the rights of minorities be considered?' the simple answer is that all can be settled by the people. The Reformers of 1832 did not map out the details of the new government of England; they simply gave the power to the people, and the people rooted out abuses and reformed the administration of law. It will be sufficient to-day if the people are admitted to that place in Church government which is now usurped by the clergy or their nominees. The State is democratic, the Church must also be democratic. As the State is governed by the people for the people, the Church must be governed by the people for the people.

It is waste of time to make a paper constitution,

which often binds the hopes of its makers to one plan. Church boards, a popular veto on patronage, or a general synod, may be the best means of introducing the people's power, but it is not wise to proceed as if the means were ends. Church reformers need not advocate any means as essential, the one thing essential is to give the people power to form their own Church; to see, in a word, that the Church is the people's Church.

The obstacle to Church reform is not the doubt as to its possibility or difference of opinion as to its method. The real obstacle is the general indifference to religion. The zeal or enthusiasm which passes as religious is most often roused by opinions, and, as Wesley said, ' Zeal for opinions is not zeal for religion.' In the noise of controversy and in the hurry of trade the very nature of religion seems forgotten. The arguments of theologians and the sensationalism of revivalists are discussed as religious problems, in which it is well to show an intelligent interest, but men do not feel that their daily lives, the lives of the poor, and the hope of England depend on their relation with God. If it were really seen that it is on religion, that is, on keeping up the communication between the little good within and the great good without, between man's broken light and God's full light, that trade, happiness, and life depend; if it were seen that England cannot be virtuous till Englishmen drink of the Fountain of virtue, then Church reform would be undertaken without delay. No difficulty would seem too great to prevent the vast resources of the Church being brought to the service of religion, and the highest intelligence of statesmen would be devoted to making perfect the organisation for spiritualising life.

It may not be in the power of those of less intelligence to tell the method of reform, but all who are weary at the thought of the present condition of the people may refresh themselves with hopes. Those who reflect on the cheerless faces so common to East London, the dull, weary round of the workers, their deathful life and their hopeless death, are borne down by the thought that each lives in the parish of some Church minister. They weary themselves wondering how the servant provided by the State might better serve the needs of the poor, how the great Church organisation might eradicate unfit houses, bring wealth to the relief of poverty, and make the means of joy more equal. They ask themselves in vain how the house of God might be a house for God's children. Unable to answer, they may at any rate gladden themselves with an ideal.

The People's Church then may be so close to the best thought of the nation that it will reflect that thought in every parish, as the ministers who have gathered light from the greatest teachers of science and history direct that light on to the lives of the hardest workers. It may be so near to every individual that its buildings will be the meeting-place of all, the scene of the Holy Communion, where men will learn to know and love God and man. It may so bring together rich and poor, the cultured and the ignorant, that the efforts and the money now fitfully wasted by rival philanthropists will be directed to the effectual remedy of ignorance and poverty. The ministers of the People's Church may be near to God and near to men, a means by which the avenues to the highest are kept open, the spiritual teachers who, by their lives and doctrines, touch the divine within the human, and make all men respond to the call of right and duty, and settle life on eternal calm.

The conception of such a Church is possible, though it is not possible to say how it may be accomplished; or how these competing claims of creeds and rituals to be religion may be satisfied; or how the rights of men and the rights of their little systems may be sunk in the thought of duty. The organisation of the Church of the future is not now to be sketched. The first step which it is for this generation to take has been made clear. All progress has been through the people, and the Church must be in fact, as in name, the people's Church. There must be a parish parliament and not a parish despot, and the government of the Church must be by the people as well as for the people.

This is the first step, and what will follow is in God's counsels. It is the people who govern the nation and decide on peace or war. They have moulded the machinery by which justice is administered and freedom secured; the people must also mould the machinery by which right will be taught and life spiritualised. If they are excluded from exercising their will upon the Establishment, nothing can hinder them from destroying it. God speaks in every age; He has not forgotten to be gracious, and the people are now His instruments, as in old days were kings. It is by them His will is being done, and in that belief the people may be trusted so to order the Church that by its means the Holy Spirit will once more show among men the fruit of virtue and honesty.

SAMUEL A. BARNETT.

X.

WHAT HAS THE CHARITY ORGANISATION SOCIETY TO DO WITH SOCIAL REFORM?[1]

I FEEL not a little shy at speaking to so large and thoughtful a body of workers; and I should not have ventured to accede to Mr. Loch's proposal had I not felt myself to be an old friend of the Charity Organisation Society. I cannot say that I have ever seen its founder, neither was I present at its birth, but I was at its christening, when some long names were given; and later, at its confirmation, I heard the duty undertaken, and indeed the declaration made, that the main object of its existence was 'to improve the condition of the poor.'

I am very proud of our friend; but, being a Charity Organiser, I can see his faults, of which, to my mind, one of the chief is that he has forgotten his baptism! I do not mean his name, but some of the promises then made for him. Far from forgetting his name, he thinks rather too much of it, having fallen into the aristocratic

[1] A Paper read at a meeting of members of the Charity Organisation Society, held at the Kensington Vestry Hall on February 28, 1884.

fault of believing a name more important than a character; and inasmuch as 'on what we dwell that we become,' he has run the danger—and we will not say wholly escaped it—of sacrificing the one to the other. He has, in short, unkindly ignored the thoughts and wishes of some of his god-parents. Have not his friends a right to be aggrieved?

We hear nowadays much about Social Reform, which, being interpreted, means, I suppose, the removal of certain conditions in and around society which stand in the way of man's progress towards perfection.

Every human being, surely, ought to be able to make a free choice for good or evil. It is, no doubt, possible for each of us to choose the higher or the lower life 'in that state of life in which it has pleased God to call us'; but the condition of some states keeps the higher life very low.

The moralists may tell about the educating influence of resistance to temptations; but are not temptations strong enough in themselves without being buttressed by conditions? Even the most ingenious of Eve's apologists has never ventured to advance the view that she was hungry.

It should be a matter of man's free will alone that determines which life he lives. Social conditions, over which as an individual he has no power, now too often determine for him, for there are forces in and around society which crush down the individual will of man and which bind his limbs so tightly that not only his course, but too often his gait, has been determined for him.

1. Great Wealth. Can a man live the highest life

whose abundance puts out of daily practice the priceless privilege of personal sacrifice — from whom effort is undemanded—whose floors are padded should he chance to fall—whose walls, golden though they be, are dividing barriers, high and strong, between him and his fellow-men?

2. **Great Poverty.**—Can a man live the highest life when the preservation of his stunted, unlovely body occupies all his thoughts—from whose life pleasure is crushed out by ever-wearying work—to whom thought is impossible (the brain needs food and leisure to set it going)—to whom knowledge, one of the prophets of the nineteenth century and a revealer of the Most High, is denied?

3. **Unequal Laws.**—Is a man wholly unfettered in his choice of life when his country's laws have allowed him to become a victim to unsanitary dwellings—when they permit him to sin, by providing that his wrong should (on himself) be resultless—when its ministers of justice, interpreting its laws, declare in the strong tones of action that bread-stealing is more wicked than wife-beating? Or is the highest life made more possible by laws that allow so much of our great mother earth —God-blessed for the use of mankind—to be reserved for the exclusive benefit and enjoyment of the upper classes?

4. **Division of Classes.**—Love is the strongest force in the universe. At least the ancient teachers thought so when they renamed God, and left Him with the Christian name of Love. But love, a certain kind of love for which no other makes up, becomes impossible by the great division between classes. We cannot love

what we do not know; it is as the American said, 'Oh, Jones! I hate that fellow.' 'Hate him?' asked his friend; 'why, I did not think you knew him.' 'No, I don't,' was the reply; 'if I did, I guess I shouldn't hate him.' The division between classes is a wrong to both classes. The poor lose something by their ignorance of the grace, the culture, and the wider interests of the rich; the rich lose far more by their ignorance of the patience, the meekness, the unself-consciousness, the self-sacrifice, and the great strong hopefulness of the poor.

5. Besides these conditions, others exist, forming barriers and hindering a man from leading his true life, such as want of light, space, and beauty. The sun-rising is to a large number of town livers only an intimation—and rarely an agreeable one—that they must get out of bed. It is but the lighting of a lamp, and not, as Blake said, the rising of an innumerable company of the heavenly host consecrating the day to duty by crying, 'Holy, Holy, Holy, Lord God Almighty.' And even if there is the space to see the sky, there is still the absence of leisure to watch its unhurried changes. We all haste and rush, we hurry and drive. The very parlance of the day adopts new words to express dispatch, and one dear old body whom I know, who is sixty years old and of appropriate proportions, constantly informs me that she 'flew' hither and thither—a method of locomotion which, in earlier years, I remember, she reserved strictly for future and more heavenly purposes.

But enough has been said of the ills of society. We all know them. The hearts of some of us have been very sick for many a weary year. The hands of those who have sat on the height and watched the progress of the battle have become tired, and have been upheld only by faith and prayer. But reinforcements have arrived; friends for the poor have arisen; from all sides press forward willing volunteers, who say, 'Put us in our place. Let us do something. How can we break down these barriers —unloose the golden fetters of these imprisoned souls—or relieve the burdened shoulders of those pale dungeoned creatures? How are we to make strength out of union—to right wrongs, and give to every man the light by which to see to make his choice?'

If one is to carry heavy weights one must have trained muscles. If one is to reply one must know. The Charity Organisation Society is the watchman set on a hill, who by his very constitution has special facilities for giving an answer—and a wise one—to these questions. He has exceptional opportunities for knowing both the classes in which social reform is most needed, and knows them under the best conditions. The rich come to him with 'minds on helpfulness bent'; the poor come at a time when their hearts are sore, when their lives are troubled, when their sorrows have made them 'unmanfully meek,' and they are willing to lay their lives and circumstances bare to inquiring eyes. For fifteen years the one class has been meeting the other in the thirty-nine district offices provided by the Society, and some 230,000 families have asked for succour when they have been either morally, physically, or circumstantially sick. Last year alone 14,132*l.* passed through the hands of this Director of Charity, and at this moment there are more than 2,000 men and women actively engaged in his work, while he records the names of nearly 3,000 subscribers whose money is an earnest of sympathy and potential working power.

But magnificent as this sounds, and *is* (for there can be no doubt about it that our friend is a very fine fellow), still there are flaws both in his past and present constitution and character which make his work less effective than it otherwise might be. Briefly, his heart is not large enough for his body—his circulation is slow—his movements are ponderous and, being slightly hard of hearing, he does not take in things until some little time after other people have done so. Then, too, he is somewhat a creature of habit; his mind does not readily assimilate new ideas, and he does rather an unusual number of things because 'he always has done so.' His *raison d'être*, his whole work, is founded on the first word of his name—Charity—(which the new translators tell us we may call love, if we like), and yet he is sometimes curiously persistent in 'thinking evil,' and he hardly, I fear, 'hopeth all things,' nor yet lives up to his standard of 'never failing'; or what does 463 cases thrown aside as 'undeserving and ineligible' mean in this last month's returns of work?

Then he has an odd way of talking about his work. I have often seen ordinary, commonplace, every-day sort of people begin to listen to him with keen interest, but gradually drop eyelids and lose sympathy as he threads his way through investigations, organisations, registrations, co-operations, applications, administrations, each and all done by multiplication!

This is a pity, for of course the every-day sort of people are most wanted to help him. He cannot only work with people who have been cradled in blue-books and nourished with statistics, nor yet with those who are like the man who 'did not care to look unless he could see the future.'

Some people dislike this faulty creature very much. They see no good in him, and call him all sorts of hard names; but then one is apt to find faults in large people more unbearable than in little ones. Clumsy people, if big, are so very clumsy; they tumble over the furniture, and kick the pet dog, and if they do chance to tread on toes it hurts so very much! and that is partly the case with him. But he has virtues, and plenty of them; he is not afraid of work, and he really cares for the poor; he is exceedingly honourable about money; he is methodical and business-like; he is thorough in all he does, thinking no detail beneath his notice; he is accurate about his facts and moderate in his statements; he is most even in his temper (though personally I should like him better if I could once see him in a rage), and he is patient and painstaking; he is humble, though conceited, too; that is, with the sort of conceit that one sometimes meets with in swimmers who know that they do the stroke 'quite perfectly' but yet are somewhat afraid of deep water; fearful, not of their breath or strength failing, but of the cramp, or jelly-fish, or other unknown dangers of the deep.

But that he is a fine being we shall all agree, with a full, rich nature; and if he could or would add to his many virtues that of adaptability; if he would become a little more elastic in his fingers as well as in his body; if he would take digitalis, in the shape of hearty hand-shaking, to improve his circulation; if he would determine every week to do some new thing, 'just for a change'; if he would, having been awakened by all his baptismal names, remind himself—just while he was dressing—of the main object of his existence; if he would not be above using an ear-trumpet, particularly on those occasions when he leaves his papers and goes to 'sup sorrow with the poor' —if he would do some or all of these things we might yet see his strong arm foremost among those who remove barriers to let in light: we might yet hear his strong voice giving out with no uncertain sound the charitable —the loving—answer to some of these soul-stirring questions.

For instance (and you will perhaps pardon me for carrying you into Committee for a few minutes), here is the case of Williamson, a man of forty, with his wife, three living children, and the recollections of the funerals of two. He is a casual dock-labourer, working when he can get work, and then only if his bad leg allows him. His wife asks for a loan to enable her to stock more fully her street-hawking basket. The father is described as a 'quiet, steady man.' The mother is a 'decent woman.' The decision of the Committee is 'ineligible,' and Williamson goes away a sadder and no wiser man.

And why is the case ineligible? Because the Committee think that money will do the family no good. The people are below the stage when money help can be useful. They have drifted till they are, in fact, ineligible for what the Society, materialistic as the age which counts money the greatest good, feels itself alone able to give, and by the decision of the Committee they are allowed to drift still. And yet not one of us could say that this family did not need help. On the case-paper, in the very middle of the first page, stand two *helpable* facts. Williamson is only casually employed by a great permanent company. Williamson is in no club.

Charitable *effort* needs organising even more than charitable *relief*. Some people fear the devil more than they love God ; or, in other words, they fear to do harm more than they love to do good. Seeing that money unwisely bestowed does great harm, they have hastened to organise it, neglecting meanwhile to organise effort, which for the creation of good is stronger than money for the creation of evil.

Williamson, with his rough, decent wife and his three unkempt children, is, let us grant, ineligible for charitable relief, but not for charitable effort. That might be directed to induce him to belong to a club, to take intelligent interest in the actions of his country, to realise, helped by Sir Walter Scott or Tourgénief, the thoughts of other nations, the character of other centuries or classes. Let effort be used to help him to accept the strength which union gives to resistance, be it to personal temptation or to public wrong.

And could not charitable effort undertake that Mrs. Williamson's tiring day be less degradingly tiring? Could it not provide a cosy parlour-club, or a chair more tempting than an upright Windsor, in which darning and mending would be possible ? And perhaps that dull task would not be so wholly distasteful if enlivened by a sweet voice, who would read ideas into the stitches, or sing patches into rhythmical relations. Such effort would soon make a difference in the unkempt appearance of the little Williamsons, and maybe evenings given up to those who cannot 'ask us again' or Sunday-planned walks would not be entirely wasted efforts, and if multiplied to any extent might have a perceptible influence on our country's conscience, though it might perhaps reduce our country's revenue from excise and customs.

Charitable effort, too, might make gutter-mud and street-fights less attractive to John, Sarah, and Jane by providing them with playgrounds as well as something—and perhaps young philanthropists will add somebody—to play with. And could not charitable effort take the children for a few weeks out of the one room to learn ideals of cleanliness and to have some fun which is not naughty in the cottage homes of our country villages?

And wisely directed effort might, too, aim at abolishing the system of casual labour at the docks—a system which keeps thousands of half-fed men hanging each morning about the dock gates because on one day in ten all may be wanted—a system which degrades men by forcing them to scramble for their work and almost enjoy the chance on which homes and existence depend. Such a system is not to be justified on the plea of profit or on the fear of strikes. But, granted that even my friend's great strength is powerless before Giant Dock Companies, yet is not this an occasion when, if he could do nothing else, he might use strong language, to which it is often noticed that neither animals nor companies are wholly indifferent?

So much for Williamson. But Committee is not over yet, and here are the papers of Mrs. Canty—56 years of age—a poor shrivelled old woman, ugly and uninteresting in appearance, unable to work from a dreadful complaint in her face, living with her two children, the only survivors out of a goodly family of six. The children, a boy of 20 and a girl of 16, are earning 21s. between them, and the Committee decide that the case is one 'not requiring relief.' Perhaps not—in money, but is cold, hard money the only relief that the Charity Organisation Society has to offer? Surely charitable effort could be organised for the benefit of this family. Some one could be sent with time and tact who would help the poor widow to other pleasures than those of regretful memories; for we read she was 'well-to-do in her husband's lifetime.' Some one who would make bright half-hours for her and take her mind from dwelling on her poor painful face, guiding her to draw strength from the thought of other lives and hope out of greater interests.

Is not some one's carriage at the Society's disposal in which she may be taken—she is too weak to walk and has not been out for two and a half years—to catch a glimpse of the bright spring flowers and the new-budding trees?

For the boy too. He may be in a good place and earn enough for bare necessities; but he has not the means of getting books, the opportunities for joining a gymnasium, nor the knowledge of the club, where he could be re-created and form friendships. These may all be within reach, and would certainly be for the relief of such a lad's hard and monotonous life: but the Charity Organisation Society, declaring that he does 'not require relief,' lets him go without an effort to give him what would influence his life far more radically than the asked for half-a-crown a week.

And for the girl also. She may be training for good work, but she must often be tired of the drudgery of her five years' nursing done without the help of a competent doctor—for the old lady 'doctors of herself'—and done, too, between the intervals allowed by her business of widow-cap making. Does she require no relief which the Charity Organisation Society can give—the relief which comes through books and patience-preaching pictures, the relief which follows the introduction to the singing class leading to the choir, or which comes through the hand-grasp of the wiser friend when the road is unusually drear?

Relief through such agencies would often make later relief unnecessary—relief which we *dare* not withhold, and yet ache as we silently give it to lock hospitals, reformatories, and penitentiaries. Might not—may not charitable effort be organised to remove some of the social conditions which stand as barriers to prevent, or anyhow make it painfully difficult for these eight people to live the highest, fullest, richest life?

And the hindering barriers to the rich man's life. I have hardly said a word about him, yet I am quite sorry for him, more sorry than for his poor neighbour; but there is not so much need for anyone to look after him, because he himself already does it. He had better be forgotten for a bit, so that he may be helped to forget himself. 'He that loseth his life shall find it,' and the good, if unsought, will come to him. When he, with 'all he is and has,' goes to reform his neighbour's conditions, he will find them wondrously interwoven with his own. He will find, if he digs deep enough, that the foundations of both palace and court are of the same material, and also that he both sees further and breathes easier after having melted down his golden walls to frame his neighbour's pictures.

But the Charity Organisation Society could help him.

It must help both the rich and the poor. It must make of itself a bridge by which the one set of condition-hindered people can cross to reach the other condition-hindered people; and, as is sometimes the case in fairy tales, the hindrance will in individual cases disappear in the very act of crossing the bridge.

I do not mean that the mere meeting will in itself be a social reform, but it will tend to it, and that in the best way. Which of us having once been in a court disgraceful to our civilisation, and yet all that forty or fifty families have to call 'home,' would lose a chance of promoting a Sanitary Aid Committee or of getting the law enforced or amended? Which of us, having once seen a Whitechapel alley at five o'clock on an August afternoon, and realising all it means, besides physical discomfort, could go and enjoy our afternoon tea, daintily spread on the shady lawn, and not ask himself difficult questions about his own responsibility—while one man has so much and another so little? The answer would, maybe, have legal results. Which of us, having sat by the sick-bed of the work-worn man (not having relieved ourselves by giving him a shilling), can return and drink for our pleasure the wine which might be his health? Which of us, having become acquainted with the low ideas, the coarse thoughts, the unholy hopes of (pardon the expression) the 'outcast poor,' can reject the privilege of self-sacrifice for their help; can neglect, at the cost of any personal trouble, a single effort which will aid their 'growth in grace'?

Evil is wrought from ignorance as well as want of thought; and the rich suffer from not knowing, as much as the poor from not being known. Both classes want help. They cannot alone break down their barriers, and alone they cannot live their best life. Our Society must help them—our Society, guided by wise rules as to what not to do, can introduce, as the children say, Mr. Too-Much to Miss Too-Little; it can be the 'Helpful Society,' helping the man stifled with too much; helping the man starving with too little; helping the idler whose true nature is literally ' dying for something to do '; helping the worker who seeks the grave gladly from fatigue; helping the lonely man to find his place in the crowd, and the crowd-tired man to opportunities of solitude; helping the owner of knowledge to outpour his treasures, and the ignorant to receive the same; helping the merrymaker to make merry, and the sorrowful to teach the lessons of pain; helping those who have found the true meaning of life to ring out their news to those of us who are still groping and restless for assurance: helping, in short, all who will give effort to wise uses.

Practically the thirty-nine district offices might each be the centre of all those forces which, under any name, are directed against the evils and hardships of life. Their rooms might be the places in which the members of charitable societies would hold their meetings. And, instead of dreading association with the Charity Organisation Society, all honest workers might hope to find in connection with it associates the most helpful. One day the committee-room would be occupied by a Relief Society, which would make its grants; another day would find ladies gathered to consult on some Befriending Society. Each day the office would have its charitable use, and people of all sorts would meet, thinkers and workers; the clergy and the laymen; the man with the new scheme and the well-worn worker in the old paths; the practical reformer and the enthusiast. A kind of registry might be kept by which those wanting to help might be introduced into empty posts of helpfulness. It would no longer happen that a man should be kept years at case-writing when he had within him a divine gift for managing boys. Clergymen, members of societies, by advertising their vacant posts, could then find among other societies able helpers.

Practically it seems a small thing to say, let the offices be more generously used; let the secretaries make it their business to find out the vacant posts of usefulness in clubs, night schools, &c. Such a simple practical reform might have great issues. Frequent meetings would result in action, weak local boards be strengthened, pressure brought to bear on neglectful officials, vacancies in the ranks of teachers and visitors filled, and a public opinion formed strong enough to condemn both luxury and suffering—both over and under work. If such a scope of action frightens those who are conscious of thin ranks and limited resources, let them remember that it is the thought of wider action which will tempt in recruits. Many who have no taste for 'case work' and Committee forms will be glad co-operators when, in any way, they can be brought face to face with the poor; when they can feel that, by their organised effort, some steps are being made in social reform.

I do not for a moment mean to imply that I believe society will be reformed if the Charity Organisation Society were to decide to adopt a larger policy or a more embracing area of work. Even those of us who most believe in it must acknowledge that it is but one among many influencing forces; but it is possible to hope that all such influences working together may make a community where conditions (as mountains in landscapes) will only make variety in the level of humanity. A flat country is dull. Mountains and valleys are much more beautiful; but then the hills lend their beauty to the dales—their torrents fertilise the low-lying lands, and the lofty mountain crag which first gains the light, and is the last to lingeringly let it go, gives back its reflected glory to gladden the shadowed valley.

A sameness of circumstances might not mean social reform (indeed, personally, I doubt if anything but love for God will mean social reform), but reform is necessary, and with that we all agree. 'Effort is bootless, toil is fruitless'; with that we do not agree—our very presence here denies it. There only remains then that organised effort should be directed towards reform, noticing, by the way, that, having swept the room, we do not leave the broom about! If those who make the effort will, not neglecting statistics, returns, and order, keep their eye on the far-away issue, which is the life of man raised to its perfect fulness, our children may, 'with pulses stirred to generosity,' rejoice to tell the tale of what the Charity Organisation Society did for social reform.

HENRIETTA O. BARNETT.

XI.

SENSATIONALISM IN SOCIAL REFORM.[1]

Theudas and Jesus were alike moved by the suffering of the Jews. Theudas, 'boasting himself to be somebody, drew away much people'; Jesus, who did not 'strive nor cry,' had only a few disciples, and died deserted by these.

The present method of reform is by striving and crying. The voice of those who see the evils of society is heard in the streets, and much people is drawn to meetings and demonstrations. Many, moved by what they hear, profess themselves to be 'frantic,' and the country seems ready for a moral revolt.

What shall the end be? Will the evil cease because the bitter cry of those who suffer is heard in the land? Will the 'frantic' striving of many people relieve society from the slavery of selfishness and lead to a moral reform, or will it be that after a few months some one like Browning's Cardinal will be found saying, ' I have known four-and-twenty leaders of revolt'?

This is a question to be considered, if possible, with calmness of mind, without prejudice for or against sensationalism. It may be that what seems sensational is but the bigger cry suited to a bigger world, and therefore

[1] Reprinted, by permission, from the *Nineteenth Century* of February 1886.

the only means of making known the facts which must afterwards be weighed and considered. It may be that some must be made frantic before any will act. It may be, on the other hand, that this trumpeting of sorrow and sin is the vengeance of the crime of sense, itself a sense to be worn with time; that men trumpet sorrows for mere love of noise and size, and become frantic over tales of sin to wring from each tale a new pleasure. Sensationalism in social reform is either the outcome of self-indulgence or it is the divine voice making itself heard in language which he that runs may read.

Not lightly at any rate are Midlothian speeches, 'bitter cries,' and religious revivals to be passed over. They, by striving and crying, by forcible statements and strong language, have caused public opinion to stop its course of easy satisfaction, and to express itself in new legislation. For the sake of the Bulgarians a Ministry was overturned; because of the cry of the poor an Act of Parliament has been passed; and the success of the Salvation Army has modified the services in our churches. In face, though, of these results on legislation, and of other results represented by various societies and leagues, the question still is, Will the same causes result in raising character? Professor Clifford, in one of his essays, speaks with religious fervour on the importance of character in society:—

Our words, our phrases, our forms and processes and modes of thought are common property fashioned and perfected from age to age. . . . Into this, for good or ill, is woven every belief of every man who has speech of his fellows. An awful privilege and an awful responsibility, that we should help to create the world in which posterity will live!

Further, he goes on to point out that a bad method is bad, whatever good results may follow, because it weakens the character of the doer and so weakens society.

If (he says) I steal money from any person, there may be no harm done by the mere transfer of possession; he may not feel the loss, or it may prevent him from using the money badly. But I cannot help doing this great wrong towards Man, that I make myself dishonest. What hurts society is not that it should lose its property, but that it should become a den of thieves; for then it must cease to be society. This is why we ought not to do evil that good may come; for at any rate this great evil has come, that we have done evil and are made wicked thereby.

In judging, therefore, of methods of reform it is not enough to show that laws have been passed and leagues formed; it must also be shown that the character of all concerned is raised. Jesus drew few people after Him and died alone, but He so raised the character of man that His death inaugurated a permanent reformation of society. It is as the character of men is raised that all reforms become permanent.

Oppressed nationalities depend for effectual help on the widely spread growth of sympathy with freedom; the poor will have starvation wages till the rich learn what justice requires; and religion will fail to be a power till men are honest enough to ask themselves in what they do really believe. Methods of reform are valuable just in so far as they tend to increase sympathy, justice, honesty, reverence, and all the virtues of high character. The answer, therefore, as to the end of this striving and crying of modern philanthropy is to be found in the effects which such methods have on character.

On the side of sensationalism it is urged (1) that laws and institutions are great educators. By the many laws against theft thieving has come to be regarded as the great crime, and by societies like that for the prevention of cruelty to animals kindness has come to be a common virtue. If, therefore, it is argued, by some rough awakening of the public conscience, laws have been passed and institutions started, something is done to develope the higher part of character. 'Principles,' it has been said, 'are no more than moral habits,' and if agitation leads to laws which enforce moral habits, sensationalism may thus have the credit of forming principles which make character.

It is further urged (2) that, if association be the watchword of the future and the educational force of the new age, it is by noisy means that associations must be formed, because the trumpet note which is to draw men together from parties and classes between whom great gulfs are fixed must be one loud enough to strike the senses.

Lastly, it is said (3) that many whose imagination has been made dull by the modern systems of education could never know the truth unless it were shown to them under the strongest light. They have been so rarely taught in school to take pleasure in knowledge or to stretch their minds, they have so little accustomed themselves to think over what is absent or to trace effects to causes, that it is more often by ignorance than by selfishness that they are cruel. They have been so eager in managing their inheritance of wealth that they have failed to use their other inheritance— the power of putting questions. Such people, it is argued, hearing of atrocities, learning the cost at which wealth is made, and seeing the brutal side of vice, get such development of character that they question habits, customs, conditions which they before accepted, and become more just and generous.

On the other hand, against this use of sensationalism, keeping still in view the effects on character, it is urged (1) that actions caused by the excitement of the emotions before they can be supported by reason are followed by apathy. The people who became 'frantic' at the tale of the Bulgarian atrocities have since heard almost with equanimity of suffering as terrible. The many who wrote and spoke of the bitter lot of the poor hardly give the few pounds a year required to keep alive the Sanitary Aid Society which was started to deal with what was allowed to lie nearest the root of the bitterness—the ill-administered laws of health. The leaders of the Salvation Army, pursued by this fear of apathy, have continually to seek new forms of excitement, just as politicians have to seek new cries.

Such examples seem to show that the wave which is raised by the emotions must fall back unless it is followed by the rising tide of reason, and that the effect on character of neglecting the reason is to make it unfeeling and apathetic. According to Rossetti's allegory, they who are stirred by the sight of vice become, like those who look on the Gorgon's head, hardened to stone.

> Let not thine eyes know
> Any forbidden thing itself, although
> It once should save as well as kill ; but be
> Its shadow upon life enough for thee.

The emotions, certainly, cannot be strained without loss. Of the greatest English actress it is told that she paid in old age the price of early strain on her feelings 'by weariness, vacuity, and deadness of spirit.'

It is urged further on the same side, (2) that the advertisement which is said to be necessary to promote association promotes only organisation, or that if it does promote association it fills it also with the party spirit, which is a corrupting influence.

Organisations, we have been lately told, are weakening real charitable effort. They have at once the strength and the weakness of the standing army system, they produce a body of officials keen to carry out their objects and careless of other issues, and they release individuals from the duty of serving the need they have recognised. That the sensational method of rousing the charitable activities has resulted in organisation rather than in association may be seen by reference to the Charities Register, with its long record of new societies and institutions. That it also inspires with party spirit the associations which it forms is more difficult of proof. Strong statements which are necessary to advertisement can hardly, though, be fair statements, and loud statements can rarely be exhaustively accurate. Where there is in the beginning neither fairness of feeling nor accuracy of thought there will be afterwards a repetition of the old theological hatred.

'Ye know not what spirit ye are of,' said Christ to His disciples, who, ignorant of His purpose, would have used force in His service against the Samaritans. The same party spirit still sometimes inspires those who hold grand beliefs and support great causes, the height and depth and breadth of which they have had neither time nor will to measure; and such a spirit degrades their character. It is not a gain to a man to be a Christian or a Liberal if by so doing he becomes certain that there is no right nor truth on the side of a Mohammedan or of a Tory. He has not, that is, risen to the height of his character: rather, as Mr. Coleridge says, 'He who begins by loving Christianity better than the truth will proceed by loving his own sect or Church better than Christianity, and end in loving himself better than all.' A teetotaller will not add so much to society by his temperance as he will take away from society if his character becomes proud or narrow.

Party spirit—the spirit, that is, which is roused and limited by some hasty view of truth or right—is likely to make men unjust and cruel, and so a method of reform which produces this spirit cannot be approved. In the name of the grandest causes, missionaries were in old times cruel, and philanthropists are in modern times unjust.

Lastly, (3) those who have claimed for sensationalism the parentage of some law have been met by the paradox that laws and institutions rarely exist till they have ceased to be wanted. In England public opinion condemns cruelty to animals, and so a society has been created. In Egypt, where the need is greater, but where there is no public opinion to condemn the cruelty, there is no society. Certain it is, at any rate, that the statute-book is cumbered with laws passed in a moment of moral excitement which remain without influence because they have never represented the true level of public opinion.

Where arguments are so urged for and against sensationalism it may be useful if, out of thirteen years' experience of East London life, I shortly collect what seem to be some of the effects on character developed during this period.

The first effect which is manifest is the great increase of humanity in the richer classes. This is shown not only by talk, by drawing-room meetings, and by newspaper articles, but by actual service among the poor. The number of those who go about East London to do good is largely increased. The increase is, though, I believe, greatest among those philanthropists who aim to apply principles rather than to provide relief. There have always been people of good-will ready to give and to teach; there is now an increase in their numbers, but the marked increase is among those who, following Mrs. Nassau Senior, work registry offices, on the principle that friends are the best avenues by which young girls can find places; or, following Miss Octavia Hill, become rent collectors, on the principle that the relation of landlord and tenant may be made conducive to the best good; or, following Miss Nightingale, take up the work of nursing, on the principle that the service of the sick is the highest service; or, following the founders of the Charity Organisation Society, examine into the causes of poverty, on the principle that it is better to prevent than to cure evil; or, following Miss Miranda Hill, give their talents to making beauty common, on the principle that rich and poor have equal powers of enjoying what is good; or, following Edmund Denison, come to live in East London and do the duties of citizens, on the principle that only they who share the neighbourhood really share the life of the poor. In all these cases the increase began more than thirteen years ago, and it must be allowed that the development of humanity which they represent is not of that form which can as a rule be traced to the use of sensationalism.

Another effect I notice as generally present is increase of impatience.

The richer classes seeing things that have been hidden, and ignorant that any improvement has been going on, have taken up with ready-made schemes. Irritated that the poor should find obstacles to relief in times of sickness, they, in their hurry, give the pauper a vote, but leave him to get his relief under degrading conditions. Angry that children should be hungry, but too anxious to consider other things than hunger, they start an inadequate system of penny dinners which keeps starvation alive. Stirred by the news of uninhabitable houses, and insanitary areas, and brutal offences, they pass stringent laws and take no steps to see that the laws are administered. Affected by the thought that the majority of the people have neither pleasure-ground, nor space for play, nor water for cleanliness, they raise a chorus of abuse against London government, but do not deny themselves every day the bottle of wine or the useless luxury which would give to Kilburn a park or to East London a People's Palace. Hearing that the masses are irreligious, means are supported without regard as to what must be the influence on thoughtful men of associating religion with things which are not true, nor honourable, nor lovely, nor of good report.

On all sides among persons of good-will there seems to be the belief that things done *for* people are more effective than things done *with* people. There is an absence of the patience—the passionate patience—which is content to examine, to serve, to wait, and even to fail, so long as what is done shall be well done.

The same impatience which takes this shape among the richer classes is, I think, to be seen among the poorer classes in a growing animosity against the rich for being rich. Strong words and angry threats have become common. All suffering and much sin are laid at the doors of the rich, and speakers are approved who say that if by any means property could be more equally shared, more happiness and virtue would follow. Schemes, therefore, which offer such means are welcomed almost without inquiry. Artisans, roused by what they hear of the state in which their poorer neighbours live, misled often by what they see, do not inquire into causes of sin and sorrow. Scamps and idlers come forward with cries which get popular support, and the mass of the poor now cherish such a jealous disposition that, were they suddenly to inherit the place of the richer classes, they would inherit their vices also and make a state of society in no way better than the present.

There may be such a thing as a noble impatience, but the impatience which has lately been added to character of both rich and poor is not such as to make observers sanguine of the social reform which it may accomplish. The old saying is still true, 'He that believeth shall not make haste.'

The other effect on character which has become manifest is one at which I have already hinted. It is a growing disposition among all classes to trust in 'societies,' whose rules become the authority of the workers and whose extension becomes the aim of their work. Men give all their energies to get recruits for their 'army,' recognition for their clubs, and more room for their operations. 'Societies' seem thus to be very fountains of strength, and the only method of action. Bishops aim to strengthen the Church by speaking of it as a 'society,' and individual ministers try to keep their parishes distinct with a name, an organisation, and an aim which are independent of other parishes. The lovers of emigration have for the same reason grouped themselves in no less than fourteen societies, and it has seemed that even to give music to the people has required the creation of three large societies.

A 'society' has indeed taken in many minds the place of a priest, its authority has given the impetus and the aim to action, but it has tended to make those whom it rules weak and bigoted. I see, therefore, in the members of these societies much energy, but less of the spirit which is willing to break old bonds and to go on, if need be, in the loneliness of originality, trusting in God. I see much self-devotion, but more also of the spirit of competition, more of the self-assertion which yields nothing for the sake of co-operation.

If now I had to sum up what seems to me to be the effect on character of the method of striving and crying, I should say that the possible increase of humanity is balanced by increase of impatience, by sacrifice of originality, and by narrowness. Whether there is loss or gain it is impossible to say, but it will be useful, considering the end in view, to see how the most may be made of the gain and the least of the loss.

The end to be aimed at is one to be stated in the language either of Isaiah or of the modern politician. We all look for a time when there shall be no more hunger nor thirst, when love will share the strength of the few among the many, and when God shall take away tears from every eye. Or, putting the same end in other words, we all look for a time when the conditions of existence shall be such that it will be possible for every man and woman not only to live decently, but also to enjoy the fulness of life which comes from friendships and from knowledge.

For such an end all are concerned to work. Comparing the things that are with the things that ought to be, some may strive and cry, others may work silently, but none can be careless.

None can approve a condition of society where the mass of the people remain ignorant even of the language through which come thought, comfort, and inspiration. Let it be remembered that now the majority are, as it were, deaf and dumb, for the mass of the nation cannot ask for what their higher nature needs, and cannot hear the Word of God without which man is not able to live. None can approve a condition of society where, while one is starving, another is drunken; where in one part of a town a man works without pleasure to end his days in the workhouse, while in the other part of the town a man idles his days away and is always 'as one that is served.' None can look on and think that it always must be that the hardest workers shall not earn enough to secure themselves by cleanliness and by knowledge against those temptations which enter by dirt and ignorance, while many have wealth which makes it almost impossible for them to enter the kingdom of God. A time must come when men shall hunger no more, nor thirst any more, when there shall be no tears which love cannot wipe away, and no pain which knowledge cannot remove. For this end everyone who knows 'the mission of man' must by some means work.

That all may avoid the loss and secure the gain which belongs to their various methods, it seems to me that they would be wise to remember two things—(1) that national organisations deserve support rather than party organisations, and (2) that the only test of real progress is to be found in the development of character.

A national organisation is not only more effective on account of its strength and extent, but also on account of its freedom from party spirit. Its members are bound to sit down by the side of those who differ from themselves, and are thus bound to take a wider view of their work. They are all under the control of the same body which controls the nation, and they thus serve only one master. A public library, for instance, which is worked by the municipality will be more useful than one worked by a society or a company. The books will not be chosen to promulgate the doctrines of a sect so much as to extend knowledge, and its management will not be so arranged as to please any large subscriber so much as to please the people. Instead, therefore, of starting societies, it would be wise for social reformers to throw their strength into national organisations.

The Board of Guardians might thus be made efficient in giving relief. From its funds and with the help of its organisation a much more perfect scheme of emigration could be worked than by private societies whose funds are limited and whose inquiries are incomplete. The workhouse might provide such a system of industrial training as would fit the inmates on their discharge both to take and to enjoy labour. It is as much by others' neglect as by their own fault that so many strong men and women drift to the relieving officer, unable to earn a living because they have never been taught to work. The poor-law infirmary, too, properly organised under doctors and nurses and visited by ladies, might be the school of purity and the home of discipline in which the fallen might be helped to find strength. The pauper schools in which, by the service of devoted officers, education could be perfected might do better work than the schools and orphanages which depend on voluntary offerings and often aim at narrow issues. The Guardians, moreover, having the power over out-relief, have in their hands a great instrument for good or evil. Rightly used, the power gives to many who are weak a new strength, as they realise that refusal implies respect, and that a system of relief which encourages one to bluster and another to cringe cannot be good.

The School Board might, in the same way, be made to cover the aims of the educationalists. As managers of individual schools these reformers could bring themselves into close connection with teachers and children. They could show the teachers what is implied in knowledge, introduce books of wider views, and they could visit the children's homes, arrange for their holidays, and see to their pleasures. Much more important is it that the schools under the nation's control should be good than that special schools should be started to achieve certain results. In connection, too, with the Board it is possible to have night classes, which should be in reality classes in higher education, and means both of promoting friendship and gaining knowledge.

Then there are the municipal bodies, the Vestries and Boards of Works, who largely control the conditions which people of goodwill strive to improve. It rests with these bodies to build habitable houses and to see that those built are habitable, and they are responsible for the lighting and cleaning of the streets. It is in their power to open libraries and reading-rooms, to make for every neighbourhood a common drawing-room, to build baths so that cleanliness is no longer impossible, and perhaps even to supply music in open spaces. It is by their will, or rather by their want of will, that the houses exist in which the young are tempted to their ruin, and it only needs their energy to work a reform at which purity societies vainly strive.

Lastly, there is the national organisation which is the greatest of all, the Church, the society of societies, the body whose object it is to carry out the aim of all societies, to be the centre of charitable effort, to spread among high and low the knowledge of the Highest, to enforce on all the supremacy of duty over pleasure, and to tell everywhere the Gospel which is joy and peace. If the Church fulfilled its object, there would be no need of societies or of sects. If the Church fails, it is because it is allowed to remain under the control of a clerical body; its charity tends thus to become limited, its ideas of duty are affected by its organisation, and it preaches not what is taught by the Holy Spirit, who is 'the Giver of life' now as in the past, but it teaches only what its governing body remembers of the past teaching of that Spirit. All this would be changed if the people were put in the place of this clerical body. The Church would then be the expression of the national will to do good, to distribute the best and to please God.

Because the national organisations are so vast, and because association with them is the most adequate check on the growth of party spirit, it is by their means that the best work can be done. The cost involved may at times be great. It may be hard to endure the slow movement of a public body while the majority of that body is being educated; it may be bitter work for the ardent Christian to endure the officialism of a public institution; it may seem wrong that profane hands should mould the Church organisation; but the cost is well endured. The national organisations do exist, and will exist, if not for good, then for evil. They are vast, a part of the life of the nation, and the cost which is paid for association with them is often the cost of the self-assertion which, if it sometimes is the cause of success, is also the cause of shame.

Further, at this moment when many methods of social reform offer themselves, it seems to me that all would be wise to remember that the only test of progress is in the development of character. Institutions, societies, laws, count for nothing unless they tend to make people stronger to choose the good and refuse the evil. Redistribution of wealth would be of little service if in the process many became dishonest. A revolution would be no progress which put one selfish class in the place of another. The test, then, which all must apply to what they are doing is its effect on character, and this test rigorously applied will make safe all methods both new and old. When it is applied there will be a strange shifting of epithets. Things called 'great' will seem to be small, and efforts passed by in contempt will be seen to be greatest.

The man in East London who, judged by this test, stands among the highest is, I think, one who, belonging to no society, committed to no scheme of reform, has worked out plan after plan till all have been lost in greater plans. Years before the evils lately advertised were known, he had discovered them, and had begun to apply remedies unthought of by the impatient. He has won no name, made no appeal, started no institution, and founded no society, but by him characters have been formed which are the strength of homes in which force is daily gathering for right. The women, too, whose work has borne best fruit are those who, having the enthusiasm of humanity, have had patience to wait while they work. After ten years such women now see families who have been raised from squalor to comfort, and are surrounded by girls to whom their friendship has given the best armour against temptation.

That work of these has been great because it has strengthened character, and there are other fields in which like work may be done. Conditions have a large influence on character, and the hardships of life may be as prejudicial to the growth of character as the luxuries. They, therefore, who work to get good houses and good schools, who provide means of intercourse and high teaching, who increase the comforts of the poor, may also claim to be strengthening character. One I know who by patient service on boards has greatly changed some of the conditions under which 70,000 people have to live. He has never advertised his methods nor collected money for his system; he has simply given up pleasure and holidays to be regular at meetings; he has at the meetings, by patience and good temper, won the ear of his fellows, while by his inquiries into details and by his thorough mastery of his subject he has won their respect. A change has thus been made on account of which many have more energy, many more comfort, and many more hope.

One other I can remember who, even more unknown and unnoticed, came to live in East London. He gathered a few neighbours together, and gradually in talk opened to them a new pleasure for idle hours. They found such delight in seeing and hearing new things that they told others, and now there are many spending their evenings in ways that increase knowledge, who do so because one man aimed at providing means of intercourse and high teaching.

Those whose aim it is to reform the material conditions in which life is spent may, as well as those who teach, claim to be strengthening character, but the admission of their claims must depend on the way in which they have worked. They themselves can alone tell how far in pursuit of their aims they have forgotten the effect of their means upon character, and how those means are now represented by people whose growth they have helped or hindered. Teachers are not above reformers, and reformers are not above teachers. The people must be taught, and conditions must be changed. It is for those who teach as well as for those who try to change conditions to judge themselves by the effect their methods have on character. If striving and crying they have avoided impatience and allowed time for the growth of originality, if working silently they have indeed done something else than find faults in others' methods, they may be said to have secured the good and avoided the loss.

SAMUEL A. BARNETT.

XII.

PRACTICABLE SOCIALISM.[1]

SOME time ago I met in a tramcar a well-known American clergyman. 'Ah!' said he, 'ten years' work in New York as a minister at large made me a Christian socialist.' The remark illustrates my own experience.

Ten years ago my wife and I came to live in East London. The study of political economy and some familiarity with the condition of the poor had shown us the harm of doles given in the shape either of charity or of outrelief. We found that gifts so given did not make the poor any richer, but served rather to perpetuate poverty. We came therefore to East London determined to war against a system of relief which, ignorantly cherished by the poor, meant ruin to their possibilities of living an independent and satisfying life. The work of some devoted men on the Board of Guardians, helped by the members of the Charity Organisation Society, has enabled us to see the victory won.

In this Whitechapel Union there is no out-relief, and 'charity' is given only to those who, by their forethought

[1] Reprinted, by permission, from the *Nineteenth Century* of April 1883.

or their self-sacrifice, awaken those feelings of respect and gratitude which find a natural expression in giving and receiving presents. The result has not disappointed our hope. The poor have learnt to help themselves, and have found self-help a stronger bond by which to keep the home together than the dole of the relieving officer or of the district visitor. The rates have been saved 6,000*l.* a year, and that sum remains in the pockets of ratepayers to be spent as wages for work, and by the new system of relief the poor are not only more independent but distinctly richer. The old system of relief has been conquered, and the result we desired has been won. What is that result? With what a state of things does the new system leave us face to face?

We find ourselves face to face with the labourer earning 20*s.* a week. He has but one room for himself, his wife, and their family of three or four children. By self-denial, by abstinence from drink, by daily toil, he and his wife are able to feed and clothe the children. Pleasure for him and for them is impossible; he cannot afford to spend a sixpence on a visit to the park, nor a penny on a newspaper or a book. Holidays are out of the question, and he must see those he loves languish without fresh air, and sometimes without the doctor's care, though air and care are necessities of life. The future does not attract his gaze and give him restful hours; as he thinks of 'the years that are before' he cannot think of a time when work will be done, and he will be free to go and come and rest as he will. In the labourer's future there are only the workhouse and the grave. He hardly dares to think at all, for thought suggests that to-morrow a change in trade or a master's whim may throw him out of work and leave him unable to pay for rent or for food. The labourers—and it is to be remembered that they form the largest class in the nation—have few thoughts of joy and little hope of rest; they are well off if in a day they can obtain ten hours of the dreariest labour, if they can return to a weather-proof room, if they can eat a meal in silence while the children sleep around, and then turn into bed to save coal and light; they are well off indeed, only because they are stolid and indifferent. Their lives all through the days and years slope into a darkness which is not 'quieted by hope.'

If the wages be 40s. a week the condition is still one to depress those who on Sunday bless God for their creation. The skilled artisan, having paid rent and club money and provided household necessaries, has no margin out of which to provide for pleasure, for old age, or even for the best medical skill. There can be for him no quiet hours with books or pictures, while his children or friends make music for his solace. He can invite no friends for a Christmas dance; he can wander in the thought of no future of pleasure or of rest. England is the land of sad monuments. The saddest monument is, perhaps, 'the respectable working man,' who has been erected in honour of Thrift. His brains, which might have shown the world how to save men, have been spent in saving pennies; his life, which might have been happy and full, has been dulled and saddened by taking 'thought for the morrow.'

This ought not so to be, and this will not always be. The question therefore naturally occurs, 'Why should not the State provide what is needed?' This is the question to which the Socialist is ready with many a response. Some of his suggestions, even if good, are impracticable. It may be urged, for instance, that relief works should be started, that State workshops should be opened, and starvation made impossible. Or it may be urged that the land should be nationalised and large incomes divided. To such suggestions, and to many like them, it is a sufficient answer that they are impracticable. Their attainment, even were it desirable, is not within measurable distance, and to press them is likely to distract attention from what is possible. If a boy who goes out ' in the interest of the fox ' can spoil a hunt by dragging a herring across the scent, a well-meaning socialist may hinder reform by drawing a fair fancy across the line of men's imagination. <u>All real progress</u> must be by growth; the new must be a development of the old, and not a branch added on from another root. A change which does not fit into and grow out of things that already exist is not a practicable change, and such are some of the changes now advocated by socialists upon platforms. The condition of the people is one not to be long endured, but the answer to the question, ' What can the State do ? ' must be a practicable one, or we shall waste time, make mistakes, rouse up anarchy, and destroy much that is good.

Facing, then, the whole position, we see that among the majority of Englishmen life is poor; that among the few life is made rich. The thoughts stored in books, the beauty rescued from nature and preserved in pictures, the intercourse made possible by means of steam locomotion, stir powers in the few which lie asleep in the many. If it be true, as the poet says, that men ' live by admiration,' it is the few who live, for it is they who know that which is worth admiration.

It seems a hard thing—but I believe that it is on the line of truth—to say that the dock labourer cannot live the life of Christ; he may, by loving and trusting, live a higher life than that lived by many rich men, but he cannot live the highest life possible to men of this time. To live the life of Christ is to make manifest the truth and to enjoy the beauty of God. The labourer who knows nothing of the law of life which has been revealed by the discoveries of science, who knows nothing which, by admiration, can lift him out of himself, cannot live the highest life of his day, as Christ lived the highest life of His day. The social reformer must go alongside the Christian missionary, if he be not himself the Christian missionary.

Facing, then, the whole position, we see first the poverty of life which besets the majority of the people, and further we recognise that the remedy must be one which shall be practicable, and shall not affect the sense of independence. It is difficult to state any principle which such remedy should follow. If it be said that men's *needs*, not their *wants*, may be supplied by others' help, then it is necessary to set up an arbitrary definition and to define *wants* as those good things which a man recognises to be necessary for his life, and *needs* as those good things the good of which is unseen by the individual to whose well-being, in the interests of the whole, they are necessary. Food and clothing would thus be an example of a man's *wants*, education of his *needs*; and it might, according to this definition, be a statement of a principle to say that the remedy for the sadness of English labour is to be sought in letting the State provide for a man's needs while he is left to provide for his own wants. It is, however, a statement which, depending on an arbitrary and shifting definition, would not be understood. If, as another statement of a principle, it be said that means of life may be provided, while for means of livelihood a man must work, then it becomes difficult to draw a distinction, for some means of life are also means of livelihood. There is no principle as yet stated according to which limits of State interference may be defined.

The better plan is to consider the laws which are accepted as laws of England, and to study how, by their development, a remedy may be found. On the statute book there are many socialistic laws. The Poor Law, the Education Act, the Established Church, the Land Act, the Artisans' Dwellings Act, and the Libraries Act are socialistic.

The Poor Law provides relief for the destitute and medical care for the poor. By a system of outdoor relief it has won the condemnation of many who care for the poor, and see that outdoor relief robs them of their energy, their self-respect, and their homes. There is no reason, however, why the Poor Law should not be developed in more healthy ways. Pensions of 8s. or 10s. a week might be given to every citizen who had kept himself until the age of 60 without workhouse aid. If such pensions were the right of all, none would be tempted to lie to get them, nor would any be tempted to spy and bully in order to show the undesert of applicants. So long as relief is a matter of desert, and so long as the most conscientious relieving officers are liable to err, there must be mistakes both on the side of indulgence and of neglect. The one objection to out-relief, which is at present recognised by the poor, is that the system puts it in the power of the relieving officer to act as judge in matters of which he must be ignorant, so that he gives relief to the careless or crafty and passes over those who in self-respect hide their trouble. Pensions, too, it may be added, would be no more corrupting to the labourer who works for his country in the workshop than for the civil servant who works for his country at the desk, and the cost of pensions would be no greater than is the cost of infirmaries and almshouses. In one way or another the old and the poor are now kept by those who are richer, and the present method is not a cheap one.

Many men and women fail because they do not know how to work. The workhouses might be made schools of industry. If the ignorant could be detained in workhouses until they had learnt the use of a tool and the pleasure of work, these establishments would become technical schools of the kind most needed, and yearly add a large sum to the wealth of the nation.

Lastly, the whole system of medical relief might be so organised as to provide for every citizen the skill and care necessary for his cure in sickness. As it is, no labourer nor artisan is expected to make such provision, as there are hospitals, infirmaries, and dispensaries to supply his wants. By application or by letter he can gain admission to any of these, and he is expected to be grateful. Medical relief is thus supplied; to organise the relief is merely to take another step along a path already entered, and properly organised the relief need not pauperise. The necessity of begging for a letter, the obligation of humbly waiting at hospital or dispensary doors, the chance that real needs may be unskilfully treated—these are the things which degrade a man. If all the dispensaries, hospitals, and infirmaries were properly ordered, controlled by the State, and open as a matter of right to all comers, it would be possible for every citizen at the dispensary to get the necessary advice and medicine, and thence, if he would, to enter a hospital without any sense of degradation. The national health is the nation's interest, and without additional outlay it could be brought about that every man, woman, and child should have the medical treatment necessary to their condition. The rich would still get sufficient advantage, but it would no longer happen that the lives most useful to the nation would be left to the care of practitioners who, however kind and devoted, cannot provide either adequate drugs or spare the time for necessary study when for visit and drugs the charge cannot be more than 1s. or 1s. 6d.

By some such development as these suggested, without any break with old traditions, without any fear of pauperising the people, the Poor Law might help to make the life of England healthier and more restful.

In the same way the Education Act might be developed in conjunction with the Church and the Universities to make the life of England wiser and fuller. A complete system of national education ought to take the child from the nursery, pass him through high schools to the University, and then provide him with means to develop the higher life of which all are capable. Some steps have already been made in this direction, but secondary schools or high schools are still needed, and the Church organisation will have to be made popular, so as to represent, not the opinions of a mediæval sect, but the opinions of nineteenth-century Englishmen. Schools in which it would be possible to learn the facts and thoughts new to this age, Churches in which, by ministers in sympathy with their hearers and by the use of forms native of the times, men could be lightened with light upon their souls, would add an untold quantity to the sum of national life.

Alongside of such development much might be done with the Libraries Act and with the powers which local bodies have to keep up parks and gardens. It would be as easy to find in every neighbourhood a site for the people's playground as it is for the workhouse, and all might have, what is now the privilege of the rich, a place for quiet, the sight of green grass and fair flowers. It would be as easy to build a library as an infirmary. In every parish there might be rooms lighted and warmed, where cosy chairs and well-filled shelves might invite the weary man to wander in other times and climes with other mates and minds. In every locality there might be a hall where music, or pictures, or the talk of friends would call into action sleeping powers, and by admiration arouse the deadened to life. The best things gain nothing by being made private property; a fine picture possessed by the State will give the individual who looks at it as much pleasure as if he possessed it. It is no idle dream that the Crystal Palace might become a national institution, open free for the enjoyment of all, dedicated to the service of the people, for the recreation of their lives, by means of music, knowledge, and beauty.

If still it be said that none of these good things touch the want most recognised, the need of better dwellings, then we have in the Artisans' Dwellings Act a law which only requires wise handling to be made to serve this purpose. A local board has now the power to pull down rookeries and to let the ground at a price which will enable honest builders to erect decent dwellings at low rents. Unwisely handled, the law may only destroy existing dwellings and put heavy compensation into the pockets of unworthy landlords and fees into those of active officials; wisely handled, the same law might at no very great expense replace the houses which now ruin the life of the poor and disgrace the English name.

Thus it is—and other laws, such as the Irish Land Act, are open to the same process of development—that without revolution reform could be wrought. I can conceive a great change in the condition of the people, worked out in our own generation, without any revolution or break with the past. With <u>wages at their present</u> rate I can yet imagine the houses made strong and healthy, education and public baths made free, and the possibility of investing in land made easy. I can imagine that, without increase of their private wealth, the poor might have in libraries, music-halls, and flower gardens that on which wealth is spent. I can imagine the youth of the nation made strong by means of fresh air and the doctor's care, the aged made restful by means of honourable pensions. I can imagine the Church as the people's Church, its buildings the halls where they are taught by their chosen teachers, the meeting-places where they learn the secret of union and brotherly love, the houses of prayer where in the presence of the Best they lift themselves into the higher life of duty and devotion to right—all this I can imagine, because it is practicable. I cannot imagine that which must be reached by new departures and so-called Continental practices. Any scheme, whatever it may promise in the future, which involves revolution in the present is impracticable, and any flirting with it is likely to hinder the progress of reform.

But now there rises the obvious objection, 'All this will cost much money;' 'Free education means 1*d*. in the pound; libraries and museums mean 2*d*.;' 'The suggested changes would absorb more than 1*s*.; the ratepayers could not stand it.'

I agree; the present ratepayers could not pay heavier rates. There must be other means of raising the money. Some scheme for graduated taxing might be possible; but perhaps I may be told that such a scheme means the introduction of a new principle, and is as much outside my present scope as the scheme for nationalisation of the land. Well, there remains the wealth locked up in the endowed charities, the increase which would be brought to the revenue by a new assessment of the land-tax, and the sum which might be saved by abolishing sinecures and waste in every public office.

The wealth of the endowed charities has never been realised, and if that amount be not reduced in paying for elementary education, it might do much to make life happier. If men saw to what uses this money could be put, they would not be so ready to back up an agitation raised on the School Board to get hold of this money for School Board work. They would say, 'No; the schools are safe; in some way they must be provided and paid for. We won't shield the Board from attacks of rate-payers by giving them our money to spend; we want that for things which the board cannot provide.' There is also a vast sum which might be got by a new assessment—which in some cases would be a re-imposition—of the land-tax, and by a closer scrutiny into the ways of public offices. The land-tax returns the same amount as it returned more than two hundred years ago, while rents have gone on increasing. The abuses of sinecures and of useless officials are patent to all who know anything of public work in small areas; and it is possible that what is done in the vestry, on a small scale, is developed by the atmosphere of grander surroundings into grander proportions. The parish reformer can put his finger on one or two officials who are not wanted, but whose salary of a few hundreds seems hardly worth the saving; perchance the parliamentary reformer might put his finger on unnecessary officials whose salaries amount to thousands. Out of the sums thus gained or saved a great fund could be entrusted to the governing body of London, and the responsibility would then lie with the electors to choose men capable of administering vast wealth, so as to give to all the means of developing their highest possibilities.

Perhaps, though, it is unwise to go into these details and attempt to show how the necessary money may be raised. In England poverty and wealth have met together. It is the fellow-citizens of the poor who see them in East London without joy and without hope. The money which is wasted on fruitless pleasures and fruitless effort would be sufficient to do all, and more than has been suggested in this paper. There is no want of the necessary money, and much is yearly spent—some of it in vain—on efforts on societies or on armies, which promise to save the people. When it is clearly seen that wealth may provide some of the means by which their fellow-countrymen may be saved from dreariness and sickness if not from sin, then the difficulty as to the way in which the money may be raised will not long hinder action.

The ways and means of improving the condition of the people are at hand. It is time we gave up the game of party politics and took to real work. It is time we gave up speculation and did what waits the doing. Here are men and women. Are they what they might be? Are they like the Son of Man? How can they be helped to reach the standard of their manhood? That is the question of the day; before that of Ireland, Egypt, or the Game Laws. The answer to that question will divide, by other than by party lines, the leaders of men. He who answers it so as to weld old and new together will be the statesman of the future.

Samuel A. Barnett.

XIII.

THE WORK OF RIGHTEOUSNESS.[1]

'If I find ... fifty righteous within the city, then I will spare all the place for their sakes.' *Genesis* xviii. 26.

My first thought, as I face you this evening, is of your variety—of your different classes and creeds, of your various communities, and your various views. My second thought is of your common object, of the one longing—the voice of your real selves—which converts variety into unity. You would save the city. Like Abraham, you have seen doom impending; like Buddha, you have seen sights in your daily walk which make the life of ease impossible. You have met poverty, ignorance, and sin.

You have met Poverty. You know families whose weekly income is under the price of a bottle of good wine; men dwarfed in stature, crippled in body, the inmates of a hospital for want of sufficient food; women aged and hardened, broken in spirit because their homes are too narrow for cleanliness or for comfort; children who die because they cannot have the care which preserves the children of the rich.

---

[1] A sermon preached on Advent Sunday, November 27, 1887, at St. Jude's Church, Whitechapel, before a body of men and women engaged in the work of social reform.

You have met Ignorance. You know men and women gifted with divine powers, powers of clear sight and deep feeling, you have seen such people taking shallow rhetoric for reason, delighting in exaggeration, clamouring for force as a remedy, adopting swindlers as leaders, making a game—a Sunday afternoon's excitement—of matters which should tear their hearts, killing time which might have been fruitful in thought and joy and love. 'The future belongs to the man who refuses to take himself seriously,' says the mocking philosopher. The ignorance which accepts the teaching, and which goes with a light heart to agitate or to repress agitation, is a sight to destroy anyone's ease of mind.

You have met Sin, the degradation which comes of selfishness. In West London it often hides under fine trappings. Culture covers a multitude of sins. In the exquisitely ordered banquet intemperance and self-indulgence are unnoticed; in the phraseology of the office greed and selfishness pass as political economy; and in the polished talk of books and of society impurity loses its true colour. You, though, are familiar with East London, and here you see sin without its trappings; you know that intemperance—over-eating and over-drinking—means a brutalised nature; you know that greed is cruelty, and that impurity is destructive both of reason and of feeling. You have seen the victims of sin, that drunkard's home, the gambler's hell, and the sweater's shop. You know that the wages of sin is death, and that no culture can give to Mammon any nobility or warm his heart with any spark of unselfish joy.

Poverty, Ignorance, Sin—these threaten the city. Your common longing is to avert its doom. Our fathers nourished a like longing. They hoped in Free Trade, the Suffrage, the National Education, and they have been disappointed.

Free Trade has, indeed, greatly increased wealth; the number of the comfortable has been multiplied, but it is a question whether, in the same proportion, the number of the uncomfortable has not also been multiplied. Our England is larger than the England of fifty years ago, but a larger body—like a giraffe's throat —may only provide a larger space for pain! At any rate, Free Trade, which has given us cheap bread, has *not* solved the problem of the unemployed.

The extension of the Suffrage, again, for which our fathers strove, has had good results; but the example of later parliaments and the growing tendency to legislate by demonstration hardly justifies their hopes. Our fathers held that the possession of the Suffrage would be effective to destroy Ignorance; they thought that responsibility would develop the seriousness which is necessary to knowledge. They—like other good men who need God's forgiveness—fed Ignorance with abuse of opponents; with exaggerations, with party cries, they bribed Ignorance to establish its own executioner; and now Ignorance is too much puffed up by flattery, too much enriched by bribes, to yield to the voice which from the register and polling booth says, 'England expects every man' to vote according to his conscience, and then to submit to the common will.

Lastly, the passing of the Education Act seemed to many to be the beginning of a new age. Schools were rapidly built, money was freely voted, and the children were compelled to attend. The Education Act has not, however, taught the people what is due to themselves or to others. Greed is not eradicated because its form is changed, and, though criminals may be fewer, gambling is as degrading as thieving, and oppression legally exerted over the weak is as cruel as the illegal blow. The children do not leave school with the self-respect born of consciousness of powers of heart and brain and hand, nor with the humanity born of knowledge of others' burdens. It seems, indeed, as if their chief belief was in the value of competition, and their chief aptitude a skill in satisfying an inspector with the least possible amount of work. At any rate, at the end of twenty years, when a generation has been through the schools, our streets are filled with a mob of careless youths, and our labour market is overstocked with workers whose work is not worth 4*d*. an hour.

Poverty, Ignorance and Sin threaten the city. Free Trade, the Suffrage, the Education Act have been tried, and the doom still impends. What is to be done? The principle of true action lies, I think, imbedded in the old Jewish tale. It is not laws and institutions which save a city—it is persons. Institutions are good, just in so far as they are vivified by personal action; laws are good just in so far as they allow for the free play of person on person. There may be need of reform in institutions and in laws, so as to give to all an open career and equality of opportunity, but it is persons who save; and if to-day fifty—a company of righteous—men could be found in London, the city might be spared and saved.

In support of this position I would offer two considerations. (1) The common mind is now scientific. Professor Huxley, in summing up the results of fifty years of science, claims the creation of a new habit of thought as a greater achievement than any material invention. The common man in the street no longer expects a miracle or worships a theory as men once worshipped the theory of social contract; he asks for a fact. The fact, therefore, that a neighbour is righteous does most to extend righteousness. He who knows a just man is likely to give a fair day's wage and do a fair day's work, to live simply and tell the truth, and it is bad pay and bad work, luxury and lying, which do most to make poverty. He who knows a wise man is likely to search after what is hidden in thought and things, and it is carelessness of what is out of sight which makes ignorance. He who knows a good man is likely to have a passion for honour, for purity, for humanity, and it is the want of higher passion which makes sin.

The righteous man is in a real sense the master of the city. He, as Browning says, who 'walked about and took account of all thought, said and acted' was ' the town's true master.' Were there in London a company of such righteous men, the power of Poverty, Ignorance, and Sin would be broken.

(2) I am often led to observe that taste is more powerful than interest. People remain on in situations, hold opinions, and adopt habits which are against their interests, because they are more in accordance with their tastes. They *like* the surroundings, they *like* the life, and liking is an armour which resists the strong lance of the economist. Now why is it that taste overpowers interest, and that habit is stronger than law? It is because taste comes through persons and is spread by

contact. The habits or tastes, therefore, which lie at the root of Poverty, Ignorance, and Sin may best be met by the formation of other habits, which come through the example of persons, by the contact of man with man. Righteous men are therefore necessary—men who would live simply and share their luxury, whose gain would not mean another's loss, who would work for their bread, who would do justice on wrong-doers, show mercy to the weak, and walk humbly before God. The habits of respectable people, the waste, the idleness, the sensuousness are writ large in the poverty, ignorance, and sin of the disreputable. Fifty—a company of righteous men, rich or poor, setting an example of generosity and honesty, living Christ's life in contact with others—might create habits in them which would take the place of the old bad habits.

The question is sometimes asked, What has been the secret of the success of Christianity? Its basis is not a system but a life. Jesus, the Righteous One, drew to Himself the righteous. They that loved the light came to the light and found the universe instinct with life. Like leaven, the disciples leavened the mass. Christianity, in distinction from other systems, gives no scheme of belief and promises no paradise of plenty—it says instead, 'The kingdom is within you.' 'When you do right you have all that God can give.' 'The joy of Christ's is the highest joy, and His is the joy of the righteous.' Christianity spreads, if it spreads at all, by pointing to a life.

To you, then, desiring to save the city, I take up the lesson as old as Abraham and illumined in Christ. I say, 'Be righteous.'

> Follow the light and do the right,
>   For man can half control his doom,
>   Till you find the deathless angel
>   Seated in the vacant tomb.

Now, as once more I look at you, I am conscious of you not only as fellow-workers seeking a common end, but as our friends. I remember how one has sorrow, another joy, and another pain; I know the anxiety which besets those whose dear ones are in danger, and the failing of heart which comes with age. I go farther, I remind you that I know some of your shortcomings, the impatience and the indolence, the will worship and the weakness, the too great speech and the too great silence. I think I know the difficulties of some as I am sure I know the goodwill of all of you. Remembering, then, that some are sad and some are tried, I say again, 'Let everyone do that which he knows to be right.' This implies self-examination, the deliberate questioning, 'What do I think?' 'What am I doing?' This means that everyone must settle what is the law he ought to obey, and then see how, in word, and thought, and deed, he keeps that law. Before the bar of conscience all must plead guilty, and by its judgment some will have to give up pleasures and some take up burdens.

'Thy kingdom come,' we pray. A sudden answer to that prayer would, it has been said, be like an earthquake's shock.

'Thy kingdom come.' Let it come. At once rich men would be seen hurrying from their luxurious homes to restore profits wrongly and hardly taken, and poor men would busy themselves to put good work in the place of bad work. The conventional lie on the lady's lip would become a bracing truth, and the political orator would stop his abuse to do justice to opponents. The idler would become busy, the frivolous serious, and the Church bountiful. For the pretence of work, the business about trifles, the everlasting money changing, the service of fashion, the gathering and squandering, the 'aimless round in an eddy of purposeless dust'—for these there would be work which would leave men wiser and the world cleaner. Instead of scandal there would be interchange of thought, and instead of 'bold print posters,' calm statement of fact. The drunkards would give up drink, the indolent their ease, and no one again 'would beat a horse or curse a woman.' Men would become honest and quiet, they would give up envying and strife. Time spent on foolish books and in foolish talk would be devoted to study, and all obeying the call of duty would serve the common good. Such a change in character would bring about a change in things, and could, indeed, turn the world upside down. If the rich were as generous and just as Christ, if the poor were as honest and brave as Christ, there would not be much left which Socialism could add to the world's comfort. Personal righteousness must lead to peace and plenty, and without personal righteousness peace and plenty are impossible. It is, then, for us, with our high hopes, with our common longing for the time when none shall hurt or destroy, when none shall be sad or sorrowing—it is for us to be righteous. We all know a right we do not do; whatever we do, whatever we give, whatever we are, there is more we ought to do, more we ought to give, and more we ought to be.

To-night, then, seeing the doom discernible amid the

undoubted blessings of this Jubilee year; to-night, conscious that the progress (for which we thank God) has threatenings as well as promises, I preach, 'Be righteous.' No, it is not I who preach. It is Poverty, Ignorance, Sin. It is God Himself speaking through the pity and anger raised by the sight of these things. It is God Himself speaking through the reason raised by the thought of these things. It is God, the Almighty, the 'I am,' 'Who is, and was, and will be,' who says to-night, 'Be righteous.' If fifty righteous men, with Jesus as their Master, 'feeding on Him by faith,' would form a Holy Communion, the city might be spared for their sakes.

SAMUEL A. BARNETT.

JUNE 1888.

GENERAL LISTS OF WORKS
PUBLISHED BY
Messrs. LONGMANS, GREEN, & CO.
LONDON AND NEW YORK.

HISTORY, POLITICS, HISTORICAL MEMOIRS, &c.

Abbey's The English Church and its Bishops, 1700-1800. 2 vols. 8vo. 24s.
Abbey and Overton's English Church in the Eighteenth Century. Cr. 8vo. 7s. 6d.
Arnold's Lectures on Modern History. 8vo. 7s. 6d.
Bagwell's Ireland under the Tudors. Vols. 1 and 2. 2 vols. 8vo. 32s.
Ball's The Reformed Church of Ireland, 1537-1886. 8vo. 7s. 6d.
Boultbee's History of the Church of England, Pre-Reformation Period. 8vo. 15s.
Buckle's History of Civilisation. 3 vols. crown 8vo. 24s.
Canning (George) Some Official Correspondence of. 2 vols. 8vo. 28s.
Cox's (Sir G. W.) General History of Greece. Crown 8vo. Maps, 7s. 6d.
Creighton's Papacy during the Reformation. 8vo. Vols. 1 & 2, 32s. Vols. 3 & 4, 24s.
De Tocqueville's Democracy in America. 2 vols. crown 8vo. 16s.
Doyle's English in America: Virginia, Maryland, and the Carolinas, 8vo. 18s.
— — — The Puritan Colonies, 2 vols. 8vo. 36s.
Epochs of Ancient History. Edited by the Rev. Sir G. W. Cox, Bart. and C. Sankey, M.A. With Maps. Fcp. 8vo. price 2s. 6d. each.

- Beesly's Gracchi, Marius, and Sulla.
- Capes's Age of the Antonines.
- — Early Roman Empire.
- Cox's Athenian Empire.
- — Greeks and Persians.
- Curteis's Rise of the Macedonian Empire.
- Ihne's Rome to its Capture by the Gauls.
- Merivale's Roman Triumvirates.
- Sankey's Spartan and Theban Supremacies.
- Smith's Rome and Carthage, the Punic Wars.

Epochs of Modern History. Edited by C. Colbeck, M.A. With Maps. Fcp. 8vo. 2s. 6d. each.

- Church's Beginning of the Middle Ages.
- Cox's Crusades.
- Creighton's Age of Elizabeth.
- Gairdner's Houses of Lancaster and York.
- Gardiner's Puritan Revolution.
- — Thirty Years' War.
- — (Mrs.) French Revolution, 1789-1795.
- Hale's Fall of the Stuarts.
- Johnson's Normans in Europe.
- Longman's Frederick the Great and the Seven Years' War.
- Ludlow's War of American Independence.
- M'Carthy's Epoch of Reform, 1830-1850.
- Moberly's The Early Tudors.
- Morris's Age of Queen Anne.
- — The Early Hanoverians.
- Seebohm's Protestant Revolution.
- Stubbs's The Early Plantagenets.
- Warburton's Edward III.

Epochs of Church History. Edited by the Rev. Mandell Creighton, M.A. Fcp. 8vo. price 2s. 6d. each.

- Brodrick's A History of the University of Oxford.
- Carr's The Church and the Roman Empire.
- Hunt's England and the Papacy.
- Mullinger's The University of Cambridge.
- Overton's The Evangelical Revival in the Eighteenth Century.
- Perry's The Reformation in England.
- Plummer's The Church of the Early Fathers.
- Stephens' Hildebrand and his Times.
- Tozer's The Church and the Eastern Empire.
- Tucker's The English Church in other Lands.
- Wakeman's The Church and the Puritans.

⁎ *Other Volumes in preparation.*

LONGMANS, GREEN, & CO., London and New York.

2　General Lists of Works.

Freeman's Historical Geography of Europe. 2 vols. 8vo. 31s. 6d.
Froude's English in Ireland in the 18th Century. 3 vols. crown 8vo. 18s.
— History of England. Popular Edition. 12 vols. crown 8vo. 3s. 6d. each.
Gardiner's History of England from the Accession of James I. to the Outbreak of the Civil War. 10 vols. crown 8vo. 60s.
— History of the Great Civil War, 1642-1649 (3 vols.) Vol. 1, 1642-1644, 8vo. 21s.
Greville's Journal of the Reigns of King George IV., King William IV., and Queen Victoria. Cabinet Edition. 8 vols. crown 8vo. 6s. each.
Historic Towns. Edited by E. A. Freeman, D.C.L. and the Rev. William Hunt, M.A. With Maps and Plans. Crown 8vo. 3s. 6d. each.

London. By W. E. Loftie.
Exeter. By E. A. Freeman.
Cinque Ports. By Montagu Burrows.

Bristol. By the Rev. W. Hunt.
Oxford. By the Rev. C. W. Boase.
Colchester. By the Rev. E. O. Cutts.

Lecky's History of England in the Eighteenth Century. Vols. 1 & 2, 1700-1760, 8vo. 36s. Vols. 3 & 4, 1760-1784, 8vo. 36s. Vols. 5 & 6, 1784-1793, 36s.
— History of European Morals. 2 vols. crown 8vo. 16s.
— — Rationalism in Europe. 2 vols. crown 8vo. 16s.
Longman's Life and Times of Edward III. 2 vols. 8vo. 28s.
Macaulay's Complete Works. Library Edition. 8 vols. 8vo. £5. 5s.
— — — Cabinet Edition. 16 vols. crown 8vo. £4. 16s.
— History of England:—
Student's Edition. 2 vols. cr. 8vo. 12s. | Cabinet Edition. 8 vols. post 8vo. 48s.
People's Edition. 4 vols. cr. 8vo. 16s. | Library Edition. 5 vols. 8vo. £4.
Macaulay's Critical and Historical Essays, with Lays of Ancient Rome In One Volume:—
Authorised Edition. Cr. 8vo. 2s. 6d. | Popular Edition. Cr. 8vo. 2s. 6d.
or 3s. 6d. gilt edges.
Macaulay's Critical and Historical Essays:—
Student's Edition. 1 vol. cr. 8vo. 6s. | Cabinet Edition. 4 vols. post 8vo. 24s.
People's Edition. 2 vols. cr. 8vo. 8s. | Library Edition. 3 vols. 8vo. 36s.
Macaulay's Speeches corrected by Himself. Crown 8vo. 3s. 6d.
Malmesbury's (Earl of) Memoirs of an Ex-Minister. Crown 8vo. 7s. 6d.
May's Constitutional History of England, 1760-1870. 3 vols. crown 8vo. 18s.
— Democracy in Europe. 2 vols. 8vo. 32s.
Merivale's Fall of the Roman Republic. 12mo. 7s. 6d.
— General History of Rome, B.C. 753-A.D. 476. Crown 8vo. 7s. 6d.
— History of the Romans under the Empire. 8 vols. post 8vo. 48s.
Nelson's (Lord) Letters and Despatches. Edited by J. K. Laughton. 8vo. 16s.
Pears' The Fall of Constantinople. 8vo. 16s.
Richey's Short History of the Irish People. 8vo. 14s.
Saintsbury's Manchester: a Short History. Crown 8vo. 3s. 6d.
Seebohm's Oxford Reformers—Colet, Erasmus, & More. 8vo. 14s.
Short's History of the Church of England. Crown 8vo. 7s. 6d.
Smith's Carthage and the Carthaginians. Crown 8vo. 10s. 6d.
Taylor's Manual of the History of India. Crown 8vo. 7s. 6d.
Todd's Parliamentary Government in England (2 vols.) Vol. 1, 8vo. 21s.
Tuttle's History of Prussia under Frederick the Great, 1740-1756. 2 vols. crown 8vo. 18s.

LONGMANS, GREEN, & CO., London and New York.

Vitzthum's St. Petersburg and London, 1852-1864. 2 vols. 8vo. 30s.
Walpole's History of England, from 1815. 6 vols. 8vo. Vols. 1 & 2, 1815-1832, 36s.
  Vol. 3, 1832-1841, 18s. Vols. 4 & 5, 1841-1858, 36s.
Wylie's History of England under Henry IV. Vol. 1, crown 8vo. 10s. 8d.

BIOGRAPHICAL WORKS

Armstrong's (E. J.) Life and Letters. Edited by G. F. Armstrong. Fcp. 8vo. 7s. 6d.
Bacon's Life and Letters, by Spedding. 7 vols. 8vo. £4. 4s.
Bagehot's Biographical Studies. 1 vol. 8vo. 12s.
Carlyle's Life, by J. A. Froude. Vols. 1 & 2, 1795-1835, 8vo. 32s. Vols. 3 & 4,
  1834-1881, 8vo. 32s.
— (Mrs.) Letters and Memorials. 3 vols. 8vo. 36s.
Doyle (Sir F. H.) Reminiscences and Opinions. 8vo. 16s.
English Worthies. Edited by Andrew Lang. Crown 8vo. each 1s. sewed;
  1s. 6d. cloth.
  Charles Darwin. By Grant Allen. | Steele. By Austin Dobson.
  Shaftesbury (The First Earl). By | Ben Jonson. By J. A. Symonds.
    H. D. Traill. | George Canning. By Frank H. Hill.
  Admiral Blake. By David Hannay. | Claverhouse. By Mowbray Morris.
  Marlborough. By Geo. Saintsbury. |
Fox (Charles James) The Early History of. By Sir G. O. Trevelyan, Bart.
  Crown 8vo. 6s.
Froude's Cæsar: a Sketch. Crown 8vo. 6s.
Hamilton's (Sir W. R.) Life, by Graves. Vols. 1 and 2, 8vo. 15s. each.
Havelock's Life, by Marshman. Crown 8vo. 3s. 6d.
Jenkin's (Fleeming) Papers, Literary, Scientific, &c. With Memoir by R. L.
  Stevenson. 2 vols. 8vo. 32s.
Laughton's Studies in Naval History. 8vo. 10s. 6d.
Macaulay's (Lord) Life and Letters. By his Nephew, Sir G. O. Trevelyan, Bart.
  Popular Edition, 1 vol. crown 8vo. 6s. Cabinet Edition, 2 vols. post
  8vo. 12s. Library Edition, 2 vols. 8vo. 36s.
Mendelssohn's Letters. Translated by Lady Wallace. 2 vols. cr. 8vo. 5s. each.
Müller's (Max) Biographical Essays. Crown 8vo. 7s. 6d.
Newman's Apologia pro Vitâ Suâ. Crown 8vo. 6s.
Pasteur (Louis) His Life and Labours. Crown 8vo. 7s. 6d.
Shakespeare's Life (Outlines of), by Halliwell-Phillipps. 2 vols. royal 8vo. 10s. 8d.
Southey's Correspondence with Caroline Bowles. 8vo. 14s.
Stephen's Essays in Ecclesiastical Biography. Crown 8vo. 7s. 6d.
Taylor's (Sir Henry) Correspondence. 8vo. 16s.
Wellington's Life, by Gleig. Crown 8vo. 6s.

MENTAL AND POLITICAL PHILOSOPHY, FINANCE, &c.

Adam's Public Debts; an Essay on the Science of Finance. 8vo. 12s. 6d.
Amos's View of the Science of Jurisprudence. 8vo. 18s.
— Primer of the English Constitution. Crown 8vo. 6s.
Bacon's Essays, with Annotations by Whately. 8vo. 10s. 6d.
— Works, edited by Spedding. 7 vols. 8vo. 73s. 6d.
Bagehot's Economic Studies, edited by Hutton. 8vo. 10s. 6d.
— The Postulates of English Political Economy. Crown 8vo. 2s. 6d.

Bain's Logic, Deductive and Inductive. Crown 8vo. 10s. 6d.
    PART I. Deduction, 4s. | PART II. Induction, 6s. 6d.
— Mental and Moral Science. Crown 8vo. 10s. 6d.
— The Senses and the Intellect. 8vo. 15s.
— The Emotions and the Will. 8vo. 15s.
Crozier's Civilisation and Progress. 8vo. 5s.
Crump's Short Enquiry into the Formation of English Political Opinion. 8vo. 7s. 6d.
Dowell's A History of Taxation and Taxes in England. 8vo. Vols. 1 & 2, 21s. Vols. 3 & 4, 21s.
Green's (Thomas Hill) Works. (3 vols.) Vols. 1 & 2, Philosophical Works. 8vo. 16s. each.
Hume's Essays, edited by Green & Gross. 2 vols. 8vo. 28s.
— Treatise of Human Nature, edited by Green & Grosa. 2 vols. 8vo. 28s.
Kirkup's An Enquiry into Socialism. Crown 8vo. 5s.
Ladd's Elements of Physiological Psychology. 8vo. 21s.
Lang's Custom and Myth : Studies of Early Usage and Belief. Crown 8vo. 7s. 6d.
— Myth, Ritual, and Religion. 2 vols. crown 8vo. 21s.
Leslie's Essays in Political and Moral Philosophy. 8vo. 10s. 6d.
Lewes's History of Philosophy. 2 vols. 8vo. 32s.
Lubbock's Origin of Civilisation. 8vo. 18s.
Macleod's The Elements of Economics. (2 vols.) Vol. 1, cr. 8vo. 7s. 6d. Vol. 2, Part 1. cr. 8vo. 7s. 6d.
— The Elements of Banking. Crown 8vo. 5s.
— The Theory and Practice of Banking. Vol. 1, 8vo. 12s. Vol. 2, 14s.
Max Müller's The Science of Thought. 8vo. 21s.
Mill's (James) Analysis of the Phenomena of the Human Mind. 2 vols. 8vo. 28s.
Mill (John Stuart) on Representative Government. Crown 8vo. 2s.
— — on Liberty. Crown 8vo. 1s. 4d.
— — Examination of Hamilton's Philosophy. 8vo. 16s.
— — Logic. Crown 8vo. 5s.
— — Principles of Political Economy. 2 vols. 8vo. 30s. People's Edition, 1 vol. crown 8vo. 5s.
— — Utilitarianism. 8vo. 5s.
— — Three Essays on Religion, &c. 8vo. 5s.
Mulhall's History of Prices since 1850. Crown 8vo. 6s.
Sandars's Institutes of Justinian, with English Notes. 8vo. 18s.
Seebohm's English Village Community. 8vo. 16s.
Sully's Outlines of Psychology. 8vo. 12s. 6d.
— Teacher's Handbook of Psychology. Crown 8vo. 6s. 6d.
Swinburne's Picture Logic. Post 8vo. 5s.
Thompson's A System of Psychology. 2 vols. 8vo. 36s.
— The Problem of Evil. 8vo. 10s. 6d.
— The Religious Sentiments of the Human Mind. 8vo. 7s. 6d.
Thomson's Outline of Necessary Laws of Thought. Crown 8vo. 6s.
Twiss's Law of Nations in Time of War. 8vo. 21s.
— — in Time of Peace. 8vo. 15s.
Webb's The Veil of Isis. 8vo. 10s. 6d.
Whately's Elements of Logic. Crown 8vo. 4s. 6d.
— — Rhetoric. Crown 8vo. 4s. 6d.
Wylie's Labour, Leisure, and Luxury. Crown 8vo. 6s.
Zeller's History of Eclecticism in Greek Philosophy. Crown 8vo. 10s. 6d.
— Plato and the Older Academy. Crown 8vo. 18s.

LONGMANS, GREEN, & CO., London and New York.

Zeller's Pre-Socratic Schools. 2 vols. crown 8vo. 30s.
— Socrates and the Socratic Schools. Crown 8vo. 10s. 6d.
— Stoics, Epicureans, and Sceptics. Crown 8vo. 15s.
— Outlines of the History of Greek Philosophy. Crown 8vo. 10s. 6d.

MISCELLANEOUS WORKS.

A. K. H. B., The Essays and Contributions of. Crown 8vo.
    Autumn Holidays of a Country Parson. 3s. 6d.
    Changed Aspects of Unchanged Truths. 3s. 6d.
    Common-Place Philosopher in Town and Country. 3s. 6d.
    Critical Essays of a Country Parson. 3s. 6d.
    Counsel and Comfort spoken from a City Pulpit. 3s. 6d.
    Graver Thoughts of a Country Parson. Three Series. 3s. 6d. each.
    Landscapes, Churches, and Moralities. 8s. 6d.
    Leisure Hours in Town. 3s. 6d. Lessons of Middle Age. 3s. 6d.
    Our Homely Comedy ; and Tragedy. 3s. 6d.
    Our Little Life. Essays Consolatory and Domestic. Two Series. 3s. 6d.
    Present-day Thoughts. 3s. 6d.   [each.
    Recreations of a Country Parson. Three Series. 3s. 6d. each.
    Seaside Musings on Sundays and Week-Days. 3s. 6d.
    Sunday Afternoons in the Parish Church of a University City. 3s. 6d.
Armstrong's (Ed. J.) Essays and Sketches. Fcp. 8vo. 5s.
Arnold's (Dr. Thomas) Miscellaneous Works. 8vo. 7s. 6d.
Bagehot's Literary Studies, edited by Hutton. 2 vols. 8vo. 28s.
Beaconsfield (Lord), The Wit and Wisdom of. Crown 8vo. 1s. boards ; 1s. 6d. cl.
Farrar's Language and Languages. Crown 8vo. 8s.
Froude's Short Studies on Great Subjects. 4 vols. crown 8vo. 24s.
Huth's The Marriage of Near Kin. Royal 8vo. 21s.
Lang's Letters to Dead Authors. Fcp. 8vo. 6s. 6d.
— Books and Bookmen. Crown 8vo. 6s. 6d.
Macaulay's Miscellaneous Writings. 2 vols. 8vo. 21s. 1 vol. crown 8vo. 4s. 6d.
— Miscellaneous Writings and Speeches. Crown 8vo. 6s.
— Miscellaneous Writings, Speeches, Lays of Ancient Rome, &c. Cabinet Edition. 4 vols. crown 8vo. 24s.
— Writings, Selections from. Crown 8vo. 6s.
Max Müller's Lectures on the Science of Language. 2 vols. crown 8vo. 16s.
— — Lectures on India. 8vo. 12s. 6d.
— — Biographies of Words and the Home of the Aryas. Crown 8vo. 7s. 6d.
Oliver's Astronomy for Amateurs. Crown 8vo. 7s. 6d.
Proctor's Chance and Luck. Crown 8vo. 5s.
Smith (Sydney) The Wit and Wisdom of. Crown 8vo. 1s. boards ; 1s. 8d. cloth.

ASTRONOMY.

Herschel's Outlines of Astronomy. Square crown 8vo. 12s.
Proctor's Larger Star Atlas. Folio, 15s. or Maps only, 12s. 6d.
    — New Star Atlas. Crown 8vo. 5s.
    — Light Science for Leisure Hours. 3 Series. Crown 8vo. 5s. each.
    — The Moon. Crown 8vo. 6s.
    — Other Worlds than Ours. Crown 8vo. 5s.
    — Studies of Venus-Transits. 8vo. 5s.
    — Orbs Around Us. Crown 8vo. 5s.
    — Universe of Stars. 8vo. 10s. 6d.
    — Old and New Astronomy. 12 Parts. 2s. 6d. each. (In course of publication.)
Webb's Celestial Objects for Common Telescopes. Crown 8vo. 9s.

LONGMANS, GREEN, & CO., London and New York.

THE 'KNOWLEDGE' LIBRARY.
Edited by RICHARD A. PROCTOR.

How to Play Whist. Crown 8vo. 5s.
Home Whist. 16mo. 1s.
The Poetry of Astronomy. Cr. 8vo. 6s.
Nature Studies. Crown 8vo. 6s.
Leisure Readings. Crown 8vo. 6s.
The Stars in their Seasons. Imp. 8vo. 5s.
Myths and Marvels of Astronomy. Crown 8vo. 8s.
Pleasant Ways in Science. Cr. 8vo. 6s.
Star Primer. Crown 4to. 2s. 6d.
The Seasons Pictured. Demy 4to. 5s.
Strength and Happiness. Cr. 8vo. 5s.
Rough Ways made Smooth. Cr. 8vo. 5s.
The Expanse of Heaven. Cr. 8vo. 5s.
Our Place among Infinities. Cr. 8vo. 5s.
The Great Pyramid. Cr. 8vo. 6s.

CLASSICAL LANGUAGES AND LITERATURE.

Æschylus, The Eumenides of. Text, with Metrical English Translation, by J. F. Davies. 8vo. 7s.
Aristophanes' The Acharnians, translated by R. Y. Tyrrell. Crown 8vo. 2s. 6d.
Aristotle's The Ethics, Text and Notes, by Sir Alex. Grant, Bart. 2 vols. 8vo. 32s.
— The Nicomachean Ethics, translated by Williams, crown 8vo. 7s. 6d.
— The Politics, Books I. III. IV. (VII.) with Translation, &c. by Bolland and Lang. Crown 8vo. 7s. 6d.
Becker's *Charicles* and *Gallus*, by Metcalfe. Post 8vo. 7s. 6d. each.
Cicero's Correspondence, Text and Notes, by R. Y. Tyrrell. Vols. 1 & 2, 8vo. 12s. each.
Mahaffy's Classical Greek Literature. Crown 8vo. Vol. 1, The Poets, 7s. 6d. Vol. 2, The Prose Writers, 7s. 6d.
Plato's Parmenides, with Notes, &c. by J. Maguire. 8vo. 7s. 6d.
Virgil's Works, Latin Text, with Commentary, by Kennedy. Crown 8vo. 10s. 6d.
— Æneid, translated into English Verse, by Conington. Crown 8vo. 9s.
— — — — by W. J. Thornhill. Cr. 8vo. 7s. 6d.
— Poems, — — — Prose, by Conington. Crown 8vo. 9s.
Witt's Myths of Hellas, translated by F. M. Younghusband. Crown 8vo. 3s. 6d.
— The Trojan War, — Fcp. 8vo. 2s.
— The Wanderings of Ulysses, — Crown 8vo. 3s. 6d.

NATURAL HISTORY, BOTANY, & GARDENING.

Dixon's Rural Bird Life. Crown 8vo. Illustrations, 5s.
Hartwig's Aerial World, 8vo. 10s. 6d.
— Polar World, 8vo. 10s. 6d.
— Sea and its Living Wonders. 8vo. 10s. 6d.
— Subterranean World, 8vo. 10s. 6d.
— Tropical World, 8vo. 10s. 6d.
Lindley's Treasury of Botany. 2 vols. fcp. 8vo. 12s.
Loudon's Encyclopædia of Gardening. 8vo. 21s.
— — Plants. 8vo. 42s.
Rivers's Orchard House. Crown 8vo. 5s.
— Miniature Fruit Garden. Fcp. 8vo. 4s.
Stanley's Familiar History of British Birds. Crown 8vo. 6s.
Wood's Bible Animals. With 112 Vignettes. 8vo. 10s. 6d.
— Homes Without Hands, 8vo. 10s. 6d.
— Insects Abroad, 8vo. 10s. 6d.
— Horse and Man. 8vo. 14s.
— Insects at Home. With 700 Illustrations. 8vo. 10s. 6d.

LONGMANS, GREEN, & CO., London and New York.

Wood's Out of Doors. Crown 8vo. 5s.
— Petland Revisited. Crown 8vo. 7s. 6d.
— Strange Dwellings. Crown 8vo. 5s. Popular Edition, 4to. 6d.

CHEMISTRY ENGINEERING, & GENERAL SCIENCE.

Arnott's Elements of Physics or Natural Philosophy. Crown 8vo. 12s. 6d.
Barrett's English Glees and Part-Songs: their Historical Development. Crown 8vo. 7s. 6d.
Bourne's Catechism of the Steam Engine. Crown 8vo. 7s. 6d.
— Handbook of the Steam Engine. Fcp. 8vo. 9s.
— Recent Improvements in the Steam Engine. Fcp. 8vo. 6s.
Buckton's Our Dwellings, Healthy and Unhealthy. Crown 8vo. 3s. 6d.
Clerk's The Gas Engine. With Illustrations. Crown 8vo. 7s. 6d.
Clodd's The Story of Creation. Illustrated. Crown 8vo. 6s.
Crookes's Select Methods in Chemical Analysis. 8vo. 24s.
Culley's Handbook of Practical Telegraphy. 8vo. 16s.
Fairbairn's Useful Information for Engineers. 3 vols. crown 8vo. 31s. 6d.
— Mills and Millwork. 1 vol. 8vo. 25s.
Forbes' Lectures on Electricity. Crown 8vo. 5s.
Galloway's Principles of Chemistry Practically Taught. Crown 8vo. 6s. 6d.
Ganot's Elementary Treatise on Physics, by Atkinson. Large crown 8vo. 15s.
— Natural Philosophy, by Atkinson. Crown 8vo. 7s. 6d.
Grove's Correlation of Physical Forces. 8vo. 15s.
Haughton's Six Lectures on Physical Geography. 8vo. 15s.
Helmholtz on the Sensations of Tone. Royal 8vo. 28s.
Helmholtz's Lectures on Scientific Subjects. 2 vols. crown 8vo. 7s. 6d. each.
Hudson and Gosse's The Rotifera or 'Wheel Animalcules.' With 30 Coloured Plates. 8 parts. 4to. 10s. 6d. each. Complete, 2 vols. 4to. £3. 10s.
Hullah's Lectures on the History of Modern Music. 8vo. 8s. 6d.
— Transition Period of Musical History. 8vo. 10s. 6d.
Jackson's Aid to Engineering Solution. Royal 8vo. 21s.
Jago's Inorganic Chemistry, Theoretical and Practical. Fcp. 8vo. 2s. 6d.
Kolbe's Short Text-Book of Inorganic Chemistry. Crown 8vo. 7s. 6d.
Lloyd's Treatise on Magnetism. 8vo. 10s. 6d.
Macalister's Zoology and Morphology of Vertebrate Animals. 8vo. 10s. 6d.
Macfarren's Lectures on Harmony. 8vo. 12s.
— Addresses and Lectures. Crown 8vo. 6s. 6d.
Martin's Navigation and Nautical Astronomy. Royal 8vo. 18s.
Meyer's Modern Theories of Chemistry. 8vo. 18s.
Miller's Elements of Chemistry, Theoretical and Practical. 3 vols. 8vo. Part I. Chemical Physics, 16s. Part II. Inorganic Chemistry, 24s. Part III. Organic Chemistry, price 31s. 6d.
Mitchell's Manual of Practical Assaying. 8vo. 31s. 6d.
— Dissolution and Evolution and the Science of Medicine. 8vo. 16s.
Noble's Hours with a Three-inch Telescope. Crown 8vo. 4s. 6d.
Northcott's Lathes and Turning. 8vo. 18s.
Owen's Comparative Anatomy and Physiology of the Vertebrate Animals. 3 vols. 8vo. 73s. 6d.
Piesse's Art of Perfumery. Square crown 8vo. 21s.

LONGMANS, GREEN, & CO., London and New York.

Richardson's The Health of Nations; Works and Life of Edwin Chadwick, C.B. 2 vols. 8vo. 28s.
— The Commonhealth; a Series of Essays. Crown 8vo. 6s.
Schellen's Spectrum Analysis. 8vo. 31s. 6d.
Scott's Weather Charts and Storm Warnings. Crown 8vo. 6s.
Sennett's Treatise on the Marine Steam Engine. 8vo. 21s.
Smith's Air and Rain. 8vo. 24s.
Stoney's The Theory of the Stresses on Girders, &c. Royal 8vo. 36s.
Tilden's Practical Chemistry. Fcp. 8vo. 1s. 6d.
Tyndall's Faraday as a Discoverer. Crown 8vo. 3s. 6d.
— Floating Matter of the Air. Crown 8vo. 7s. 6d.
— Fragments of Science. 2 vols. post 8vo. 16s.
— Heat a Mode of Motion. Crown 8vo. 12s.
— Lectures on Light delivered in America. Crown 8vo. 5s.
— Lessons on Electricity. Crown 8vo. 2s. 6d.
— Notes on Electrical Phenomena. Crown 8vo. 1s. sewed, 1s. 6d. cloth.
— Notes of Lectures on Light. Crown 8vo. 1s. sewed, 1s. 6d. cloth.
— Researches on Diamagnetism and Magne-Crystallic Action. Cr. 8vo. 12s.
— Sound, with Frontispiece and 203 Woodcuts. Crown 8vo. 10s. 6d.
Unwin's The Testing of Materials of Construction. Illustrated. 8vo. 21s.
Watts' Dictionary of Chemistry. New Edition (4 vols.). Vol. 1, 8vo. 42s.
Wilson's Manual of Health-Science. Crown 8vo. 2s. 8d.

THEOLOGICAL AND RELIGIOUS WORKS.

Arnold's (Rev. Dr. Thomas) Sermons. 6 vols. crown 8vo. 5s. each.
Boultbee's Commentary on the 39 Articles. Crown 8vo. 6s.
Browne's (Bishop) Exposition of the 39 Articles. 8vo. 16s.
Bullinger's Critical Lexicon and Concordance to the English and Greek New Testament. Royal 8vo. 15s.
Colenso on the Pentateuch and Book of Joshua. Crown 8vo. 6s.
Conder's Handbook of the Bible. Post 8vo. 7s. 6d.
Conybeare & Howson's Life and Letters of St. Paul:—
    Library Edition, with Maps, Plates, and Woodcuts. 2 vols. square crown 8vo. 21s.
    Student's Edition, revised and condensed, with 46 Illustrations and Maps. 1 vol. crown 8vo. 6s.
Cox's (Homersham) The First Century of Christianity. 8vo. 12s.
Davidson's Introduction to the Study of the New Testament. 2 vols. 8vo. 30s.
Edersheim's Life and Times of Jesus the Messiah. 2 vols. 8vo. 24s.
— Prophecy and History in relation to the Messiah. 8vo. 12s.
Ellicott's (Bishop) Commentary on St. Paul's Epistles. 8vo. Corinthians I. 16s. Galatians, 8s. 6d. Ephesians, 8s. 6d. Pastoral Epistles, 10s. 6d. Philippians, Colossians and Philemon, 10s. 6d. Thessalonians, 7s. 6d.
— Lectures on the Life of our Lord. 8vo. 12s.
Ewald's Antiquities of Israel, translated by Solly. 8vo. 12s. 6d.
— History of Israel, translated by Carpenter & Smith. 8 vols. 8vo. Vols. 1 & 2, 24s. Vols. 3 & 4, 21s. Vol. 5, 18s. Vol. 6, 16s. Vol. 7, 21s. Vol. 8, 18s.
Hobart's Medical Language of St. Luke. 8vo. 16s.
Hopkins's Christ the Consoler. Fcp. 8vo. 2s. 6d.

LONGMANS, GREEN, & CO., London and New York.

General Lists of Works.

Jameson's Sacred and Legendary Art. 6 vols. square 8vo.
    Legends of the Madonna. 1 vol. 21s.
    — — — Monastic Orders 1 vol. 21s.
    — — — Saints and Martyrs. 2 vols. 31s. 6d.
    — — — Saviour. Completed by Lady Eastlake. 2 vols. 42s.
Jukes's New Man and the Eternal Life. Crown 8vo. 6s.
  — Second Death and the Restitution of all Things. Crown 8vo. 3s. 6d.
  — Types of Genesis. Crown 8vo. 7s. 6d.
  — The Mystery of the Kingdom. Crown 8vo. 3s. 6d.
  — The Names of God in Holy Scripture. Crown 8vo. 4s. 6d.
Lenormant's New Translation of the Book of Genesis. Translated into English. 8vo. 10s. 6d.
Lyra Germanica : Hymns translated by Miss Winkworth. Fcp. 8vo. 5s.
Macdonald's (G.) Unspoken Sermons. Two Series, Crown 8vo. 3s. 6d. each.
  — The Miracles of our Lord. Crown 8vo. 3s. 6d.
Manning's Temporal Mission of the Holy Ghost. Crown 8vo. 8s. 6d.
Martineau's Endeavours after the Christian Life. Crown 8vo. 7s. 6d.
  — Hymns of Praise and Prayer. Crown 8vo. 4s. 6d. 32mo. 1s. 6d.
  — Sermons, Hours of Thought on Sacred Things. 2 vols. 7s. 6d. each.
Max Müller's Origin and Growth of Religion. Crown 8vo. 7s. 6d.
  — Science of Religion. Crown 8vo. 7s. 6d.
Mensell's Spiritual Songs for Sundays and Holidays. Fcp. 8vo. 5s. 18mo. 2s.
Newman's Apologia pro Vitâ Suâ. Crown 8vo. 6s.
  — The Arians of the Fourth Century. Crown 8vo. 6s.
  — The Idea of a University Defined and Illustrated. Crown 8vo. 7s.
  — Historical Sketches. 3 vols. crown 8vo. 6s. each.
  — Discussions and Arguments on Various Subjects. Crown 8vo. 6s.
  — An Essay on the Development of Christian Doctrine. Crown 8vo. 6s.
  — Certain Difficulties Felt by Anglicans in Catholic Teaching Considered. Vol. 1, crown 8vo. 7s. 6d. Vol. 2, crown 8vo. 5s. 6d.
  — The Via Media of the Anglican Church, Illustrated in Lectures, &c. 2 vols. crown 8vo. 6s. each.
  — Essays, Critical and Historical. 2 vols. crown 8vo. 12s.
  — Essays on Biblical and on Ecclesiastical Miracles. Crown 8vo. 6s.
  — An Essay in Aid of a Grammar of Assent. 7s. 6d.
  — Select Treatises of St. Athanasius in Controversy with the Arians. Translated. 2 vols. crown 8vo. 15s.
Overton's Life in the English Church (1660-1714). 8vo. 14s.
Roberts' Greek the Language of Christ and His Apostles. 8vo. 18s.
Supernatural Religion. Complete Edition. 3 vols. 8vo. 36s.
Younghusband's The Story of Our Lord told in Simple Language for Children. Illustrated. Crown 8vo. 2s. 6d. cloth plain ; 3s. 6d. cloth extra, gilt edges.

TRAVELS, ADVENTURES, &c.

Baker's Eight Years in Ceylon. Crown 8vo. 5s.
  — Rifle and Hound in Ceylon. Crown 8vo. 5s.
Brassey's Sunshine and Storm in the East. Library Edition, 8vo. 21s. Cabinet Edition, crown 8vo. 7s. 6d. Popular Edition, 4to. 6d.

LONGMANS, GREEN, & CO., London and New York.

Brassey's Voyage in the 'Sunbeam.' Library Edition, 8vo. 21s. Cabinet Edition, crown 8vo. 7s. 6d. School Edition, fcp. 8vo. 2s. Popular Edition, 4to. 6d.
— In the Trades, the Tropics, and the 'Roaring Forties.' Cabinet Edition, crown 8vo. 17s. 6d. Popular Edition, 4to. 6d.
Crawford's Reminiscences of Foreign Travel. Crown 8vo. 5s.
Froude's Oceana; or, England and her Colonies. Cr. 8vo. 2s. boards; 2s. 6d. cloth.
— The English in the West Indies. 8vo. 18s.
Howitt's Visits to Remarkable Places. Crown 8vo. 5s.
James's The Long White Mountain; or, a Journey in Manchuria. 8vo. 24s.
Lindt's Picturesque New Guinea. 4to. 42s.
Pennell's Our Sentimental Journey through France and Italy. Illustrated. Crown 8vo. 6s.
Riley's Athos; or, The Mountain of the Monks. 8vo. 21s.
Three in Norway. By Two of Them. Illustrated. Crown 8vo. 2s. boards; 2s. 6d. cloth.

WORKS OF FICTION.

Anstey's The Black Poodle, &c. Crown 8vo. 2s. boards; 2s. 6d. cloth.
Beaconsfield's (The Earl of) Novels and Tales. Hughenden Edition, with 2 Portraits on Steel and 11 Vignettes on Wood. 11 vols. crown 8vo. £2. 2s.
Cheap Edition, 11 vols. crown 8vo. 1s. each, boards; 1s. 6d. each, cloth.

Lothair.
Sybil.
Coningsby.
Tancred.
Venetia.
Henrietta Temple.

Contarini Fleming.
Alroy, Ixion, &c.
The Young Duke, &c.
Vivian Grey.
Endymion.

Gilkes' Boys and Masters. Crown 8vo. 3s. 8d.
Haggard's (H. Rider) She: a History of Adventure. Crown 8vo. 6s.
— Allan Quatermain. Illustrated. Crown 8vo. 6s.
Harte (Bret) On the Frontier. Three Stories. 16mo. 1s.
— — By Shore and Sedge. Three Stories. 16mo. 1s.
— In the Carquinez Woods. Crown 8vo. 1s. boards; 1s. 6d. cloth.
Lyall's (Edna) The Autobiography of a Slander. Fcp. 1s. sewed.
Melville's (Whyte) Novels. 8 vols. fcp. 8vo. 1s. each, boards; 1s. 6d. each, cloth.

Digby Grand.
General Bounce.
Kate Coventry.
The Gladiators.

Good for Nothing.
Holmby House.
The Interpreter.
The Queen's Maries.

Molesworth's (Mrs.) Marrying and Giving in Marriage. Crown 8vo. 2s. 6d.
Novels by the Author of 'The Atelier du Lys':
The Atelier du Lys; or, An Art Student in the Reign of Terror. Crown 8vo. 2s. 6d.
Mademoiselle Mori: a Tale of Modern Rome. Crown 8vo. 2s. 6d.
In the Olden Time: a Tale of the Peasant War in Germany. Crown 8vo. 2s. 6d.
Hester's Venture. Crown 8vo. 2s. 6d.
Oliphant's (Mrs.) Madam. Crown 8vo. 1s. boards; 1s. 6d. cloth.
— — In Trust: the Story of a Lady and her Lover. Crown 8vo. 1s. boards; 1s. 6d. cloth.
Payn's (James) The Luck of the Darrells. Crown 8vo. 1s. boards; 1s. 6d. cloth.
— — Thicker than Water. Crown 8vo. 1s. boards; 1s. 6d. cloth.
Reader's Fairy Prince Follow my-Lead. Crown 8vo. 2s. 6d.
— The Ghost of Brankinshaw; and other Tales. Fcp. 8vo. 2s. 6d.

LONGMANS, GREEN, & CO., London and New York.

Sewell's (Miss) Stories and Tales. Crown 8vo. 1s. each, boards; 1s. 6d. cloth; 2s. 6d. cloth extra, gilt edges.

    Amy Herbert. Cleve Hall. A Glimpse of the World.
    The Earl's Daughter. Katharine Ashton.
    Experience of Life. Laneton Parsonage.
    Gertrude. Ivors. Margaret Percival. Ursula.

Stevenson's (R. L.) The Dynamiter. Fcp. 8vo. 1s. sewed; 1s. 6d. cloth.
  — — Strange Case of Dr. Jekyll and Mr. Hyde. Fcp. 8vo. 1s. sewed; 1s. 6d. cloth.

Trollope's (Anthony) Novels. Fcp. 8vo. 1s. each, boards; 1s. 6d. cloth.
    The Warden | Barchester Towers.

POETRY AND THE DRAMA.

Armstrong's (Ed. J.) Poetical Works. Fcp. 8vo. 5s.
  — (G. F.) Poetical Works:—

    Poems, Lyrical and Dramatic. Fcp. 8vo. 6s.
    Ugone: a Tragedy. Fcp. 8vo. 6s.
    A Garland from Greece. Fcp. 8vo. 9s.
    King Saul. Fcp. 8vo. 5s.
    King David. Fcp. 8vo. 6s.
    King Solomon. Fcp. 8vo. 6s.
    Stories of Wicklow. Fcp. 8vo. 9s.
    Mephistopheles in Broadcloth: a Satire. Fcp. 8vo. 4s.
    Victoria Regina et Imperatrix: a Jubilee Song from Ireland, 1887. 4to. 2s. 6d.

Ballads of Berks. Edited by Andrew Lang. Fcp. 8vo. 6s.
Bowen's Harrow Songs and other Verses. Fcp. 8vo. 2s. 6d.; or printed on hand-made paper, 5s.
Bowdler's Family Shakespeare. Medium 8vo. 14s. 6 vols. fcp. 8vo. 21s.
Dante's Divine Comedy, translated by James Innes Minchin. Crown 8vo. 15s.
Goethe's Faust, translated by Birds. Large crown 8vo. 12s. 6d.
  — — translated by Webb. 8vo. 12s. 6d.
  — — edited by Selss. Crown 8vo. 5s.
Ingelow's Poems. 2 Vols. fcp. 8vo. 12s.; Vol. 3, fcp. 8vo. 5s.
  — Lyrical and other Poems. Fcp. 8vo. 2s. 6d. cloth, plain; 3s. cloth, gilt edges.
Kendall's (Mrs.) Dreams to Sell. Fcp. 8vo. 6s.
Macaulay's Lays of Ancient Rome. Illustrated by Scharf. 4to. 10s. 6d. Popular Edition, fcp. 4to. 6d. swd., 1s. cloth.
  — Lays of Ancient Rome, with Ivry and the Armada. Illustrated by Weguelin. Crown 8vo. 3s. 6d. gilt edges.
Nesbit's Lays and Legends. Crown 8vo. 5s.
Newman's The Dream of Gerontius. 16mo. 6d. sewed; 1s. cloth.
  — Verses on Various Occasions. Fcp. 8vo. 6s.
Reader's Voices from Flowerland, a Birthday Book, 2s. 6d. cloth, 3s. 6d. roan.
Southey's Poetical Works. Medium 8vo. 14s.
Stevenson's A Child's Garden of Verses. Fcp. 8vo. 5s.
Virgil's Æneid, translated by Conington. Crown 8vo. 9s.
  — Poems, translated into English Prose. Crown 8vo. 9s.

AGRICULTURE, HORSES, DOGS, AND CATTLE.

Fitzwygram's Horses and Stables. 8vo. 5s.
Lloyd's The Science of Agriculture. 8vo. 12s.
Loudon's Encyclopædia of Agriculture. 21s.
Prothero's Pioneers and Progress of English Farming. Crown 8vo. 5s.
Steel's Diseases of the Ox, a Manual of Bovine Pathology. 8vo. 15s.
  — — — Dog. 8vo. 10s. 6d.

LONGMANS, GREEN, & CO., London and New York.

Stonehenge's Dog in Health and Disease. Square crown 8vo. 7s. 6d.
— Greyhound. Square crown 8vo. 15s.
Taylor's Agricultural Note Book. Fcp. 8vo. 2s. 6d.
Ville on Artificial Manures, by Crookes. 8vo. 21s.
Youatt's Work on the Dog. 8vo. 6s.
— — — Horse. 8vo. 7s. 6d.

SPORTS AND PASTIMES.

The Badminton Library of Sports and Pastimes. Edited by the Duke of Beaufort and A. E. T. Watson. With numerous Illustrations. Cr. 8vo. 10s. 6d. each.
    Hunting, by the Duke of Beaufort, &c.
    Fishing, by H. Cholmondeley-Pennell, &c. 2 vols.
    Racing, by the Earl of Suffolk, &c.
    Shooting, by Lord Walsingham, &c. 2 vols.
    Cycling. By Viscount Bury.
    Athletics and Football. By Montague Shearman, &c.
    Boating. By W. B. Woodgate, &c.
    Cricket. By A. G. Steel, &c.
    Driving. By the Duke of Beaufort, &c.
    ⁎ *Other Volumes in preparation.*

Campbell-Walker's Correct Card, or How to Play at Whist. Fcp. 8vo. 2s. 6d.
Ford's Theory and Practice of Archery, revised by W. Butt. 8vo. 14s.
Francis's Treatise on Fishing in all its Branches. Post 8vo. 15s.
Longman's Chess Openings. Fcp. 8vo. 2s. 6d.
Pease's The Cleveland Hounds as a Trencher-Fed Pack. Royal 8vo. 18s.
Pole's Theory of the Modern Scientific Game of Whist. Fcp. 8vo. 2s. 6d.
Proctor's How to Play Whist. Crown 8vo. 5s.
Ronalds's Fly-Fisher's Entomology. 8vo. 14s.
Wilcocks's Sea-Fisherman. Post 8vo. 6s.

ENCYCLOPÆDIAS, DICTIONARIES, AND BOOKS OF REFERENCE.

Acton's Modern Cookery for Private Families. Fcp 8vo. 4s. 6d.
Ayre's Treasury of Bible Knowledge. Fcp. 8vo. 6s.
Cabinet Lawyer (The), a Popular Digest of the Laws of England. Fcp. 8vo. 9s.
Cates's Dictionary of General Biography. Medium 8vo. 28s.
Gwilt's Encyclopædia of Architecture. 8vo. 52s. 6d.
Keith Johnston's Dictionary of Geography, or General Gazetteer. 8vo. 42s.
M'Culloch's Dictionary of Commerce and Commercial Navigation. 8vo. 63s.
Maunder's Biographical Treasury. Fcp. 8vo. 6s.
    — Historical Treasury. Fcp. 8vo. 6s.
    — Scientific and Literary Treasury. Fcp. 8vo. 6s.
    — Treasury of Bible Knowledge, edited by Ayre. Fcp. 8vo. 6s.
    — Treasury of Botany, edited by Lindley & Moore. Two Parts, 12s.
    — Treasury of Geography. Fcp. 8vo. 6s.
    — Treasury of Knowledge and Library of Reference. Fcp. 8vo. 6s.
    — Treasury of Natural History. Fcp. 8vo. 6s.
Quain's Dictionary of Medicine. Medium 8vo. 31s. 6d., or in 2 vols. 34s.
Reeve's Cookery and Housekeeping. Crown 8vo. 5s.
Rich's Dictionary of Roman and Greek Antiquities. Crown 8vo. 7s. 6d.
Roret's Thesaurus of English Words and Phrases. Crown 8vo. 10s. 6d.
Willich's Popular Tables, by Marriott. Crown 8vo. 10s. 6d.

WORKS BY MRS. DE SALIS.

Savouries à la Mode. Fcp. 8vo. 1s.
Entrées à la Mode. Fcp. 8vo. 1s. 6d.
Soups and Dressed Fish à la Mode. Fcp. 8vo. 1s. 6d.

Sweets and Supper Dishes, à la Mode. Fcp. 8vo. 1s. 6d.
Oysters à la Mode. Fcp. 8vo. 1s. 6d.
Vegetables à la Mode. Fcp. 8vo. 1s. 6d.

LONGMANS, GREEN, & CO., London and New York.

A SELECTION OF EDUCATIONAL WORKS.

TEXT-BOOKS OF SCIENCE.
FULLY ILLUSTRATED.

Abney's Treatise on Photography. Fcp. 8vo. 3s. 6d.
Anderson's Strength of Materials. 3s. 6d.
Armstrong's Organic Chemistry. 3s. 6d.
Ball's Elements of Astronomy. 6s.
Barry's Railway Appliances. 3s. 6d.
Bauerman's Systematic Mineralogy. 8s.
— Descriptive Mineralogy. 6s.
Bloxam and Huntington's Metals. 5s.
Glazebrook's Physical Optics. 6s.
Glazebrook and Shaw's Practical Physics. 6s.
Gore's Art of Electro-Metallurgy. 6s.
Griffin's Algebra and Trigonometry. 3s. 6d. Notes and Solutions, 3s. 6d.
Holmes's The Steam Engine. 6s.
Jenkin's Electricity and Magnetism. 3s. 6d.
Maxwell's Theory of Heat. 3s. 6d.
Merrifield's Technical Arithmetic and Mensuration. 3s. 6d. Key, 3s. 6d.
Miller's Inorganic Chemistry. 3s. 6d.
Preece and Sivewright's Telegraphy. 5s.
Rutley's Study of Rocks, a Text-Book of Petrology. 4s. 6d.
Shelley's Workshop Appliances. 4s. 6d.
Thomé's Structural and Physiological Botany. 6s.
Thorpe's Quantitative Chemical Analysis. 4s. 6d.
Thorpe and Muir's Qualitative Analysis. 3s. 6d.
Tilden's Chemical Philosophy. 3s. 6d. With Answers to Problems. 4s. 6d.
Unwin's Elements of Machine Design. 6s.
Watson's Plane and Solid Geometry. 3s. 6d.

THE GREEK LANGUAGE.

Bloomfield's College and School Greek Testament. Fcp. 8vo. 5s.
Bolland & Lang's Politics of Aristotle. Post 8vo. 7s. 6d.
Collis's Chief Tenses of the Greek Irregular Verbs. 8vo. 1s.
— Pontes Græci, Stepping-Stone to Greek Grammar. 12mo. 3s. 6d.
— Praxis Græca, Etymology. 12mo. 2s. 6d.
— Greek Verse-Book, Praxis Iambica. 12mo. 4s. 6d.
Farrar's Brief Greek Syntax and Accidence. 12mo. 4s. 6d.
— Greek Grammar Rules for Harrow School. 12mo. 1s. 6d.
Geare's Notes on Thucydides. Book I. Fcp. 8vo. 2s. 6d.

LONGMANS, GREEN, & CO., London and New York.

Fewitt's Greek Examination-Papers. 12mo. 1s. 6d.
Isbister's Xenophon's Anabasis, Books I. to III. with Notes. 12mo. 3s. 6d.
Kennedy's Greek Grammar. 12mo. 4s. 6d.
Liddell & Scott's English-Greek Lexicon. 4to. 36s.; Square 12mo. 7s. 6d.
Mahaffy's Classical Greek Literature. Crown 8vo. Poets, 7s. 6d. Prose Writers, 7s. 6d.
Morris's Greek Lessons. Square 18mo. Part I. 2s. 6d.; Part II. 1s.
Parry's Elementary Greek Grammar. 12mo. 3s. 6d.
Plato's Republic, Book I. Greek Text, English Notes by Hardy. Crown 8vo. 3s.
Sheppard and Evans's Notes on Thucydides. Crown 8vo. 7s. 6d.
Thucydides, Book IV. with Notes by Barton and Chavasse. Crown 8vo. 5s.
Valpy's Greek Delectus, improved by White. 12mo. 2s. 6d. Key, 2s. 6d.
White's Xenophon's Expedition of Cyrus, with English Notes. 12mo. 7s. 6d.
Wilkins's Manual of Greek Prose Composition. Crown 8vo. 5s. Key, 5s.
— Exercises in Greek Prose Composition. Crown 8vo. 4s. 6d. Key, 2s. 6d.
— New Greek Delectus. Crown 8vo. 3s. 6d. Key, 2s. 6d.
— Progressive Greek Delectus. 12mo. 4s. Key, 2s. 6d.
— Progressive Greek Anthology. 12mo. 5s.
— Scriptores Attici, Excerpts with English Notes. Crown 8vo. 7s. 6d.
— Speeches from Thucydides translated. Post 8vo. 6s.
Yonge's English-Greek Lexicon. 4to. 21s.; Square 12mo. 8s. 6d.

THE LATIN LANGUAGE.

Bradley's Latin Prose Exercises. 12mo. 3s. 6d. Key, 5s.
— Continuous Lessons in Latin Prose. 12mo. 5s. Key, 5s. 6d.
— Cornelius Nepos, improved by White. 12mo. 3s. 6d.
— Eutropius, improved by White. 12mo. 2s. 6d.
— Ovid's Metamorphoses, improved by White. 12mo. 4s. 6d.
— Select Fables of Phædrus, improved by White. 12mo. 2s. 6d.
Collis's Chief Tenses of Latin Irregular Verbs. 8vo. 1s.
— Pontes Latini, Stepping-Stone to Latin Grammar. 12mo. 3s. 6d.
Hewitt's Latin Examination-Papers. 12mo. 1s. 6d.
Isbister's Cæsar, Books I.-VII. 12mo. 4s.; or with Reading Lessons, 4s. 6d.
— Cæsar's Commentaries, Books I.-V. 12mo. 3s. 6d.
— First Book of Cæsar's Gallic War. 12mo. 1s. 6d.
Jerram's Latiné Reddenda. Crown 8vo. 1s. 6d.
Kennedy's Child's Latin Primer, or First Latin Lessons. 12mo. 2s.
— Child's Latin Accidence. 12mo. 1s.
— Elementary Latin Grammar. 12mo. 3s. 6d.
— Elementary Latin Reading Book, or Tirocinium Latinum. 12mo. 2s.
— Latin Prose, Palæstra Stili Latini. 12mo. 6s.
— Latin Vocabulary. 12mo. 2s. 6d.
— Subsidia Primaria, Exercise Books to the Public School Latin Primer.
  I. Accidence and Simple Construction, 2s. 6d. II. Syntax, 3s. 6d.
— Key to the Exercises in Subsidia Primaria, Parts I. and II. price 5s.
— Subsidia Primaria, III. the Latin Compound Sentence. 12mo. 1s.

LONGMANS, GREEN, & CO., London and New York.

A Selection of Educational Works. 15

Kennedy's Curriculum Stili Latini. 12mo. 4s. 6d. Key, 7s. 6d.
— Palæstra Latina, or Second Latin Reading Book. 12mo. 5s.
Moody's Eton Latin Grammar. 12mo. 2s. 6d. The Accidence separately, 1s.
Morris's Elementa Latina. Fcp. 8vo. 1s. 6d. Key, 2s. 6d.
Parry's Origines Romanæ, from Livy, with English Notes. Crown 8vo. 4s.
The Public School Latin Primer. 12mo. 2s. 6d.
— — — — Grammar, by Rev. Dr. Kennedy. Post 8vo. 7s. 6d.
Prendergast's Mastery Series, Manual of Latin. 12mo. 2s. 6d.
Rapier's Introduction to Composition of Latin Verse. 12mo. 3s. 6d. Key, 2s. 6d.
Sheppard and Turner's Aids to Classical Study. 12mo. 5s. Key, 6s.
Valpy's Latin Delectus, improved by White. 12mo. 2s. 6d. Key, 3s. 6d.
Virgil's Æneid, translated into English Verse by Conington. Crown 8vo. 9s.
— Works, edited by Kennedy. Crown 8vo. 10s. 6d.
— — translated into English Prose by Conington. Crown 8vo. 9s.
Walford's Progressive Exercises in Latin Elegiac Verse. 12mo. 2s. 6d. Key, 5s.
White and Riddle's Large Latin-English Dictionary. 1 vol. 4to. 21s.
White's Concise Latin-Eng. Dictionary for University Students. Royal 8vo. 12s.
— Junior Students' Eng.-Lat. & Lat.-Eng. Dictionary. Square 12mo. 5s.
Separately { The Latin-English Dictionary, price 3s.
{ The English-Latin Dictionary, price 3s.
Yonge's Latin Gradus. Post 8vo. 9s.; or with Appendix, 12s.

WHITE'S GRAMMAR-SCHOOL GREEK TEXTS.

Æsop (Fables) & Palæphatus (Myths). 32mo. 1s.
Euripides, Hecuba. 2s.
Homer, Iliad, Book I. 1s.
— Odyssey, Book I. 1s.
Lucian, Select Dialogues. 1s.
Xenophon, Anabasis, Books I. III. IV. V. & VI. 1s. 6d. each; Book II. 1s.; Book VII. 2s.

Xenophon, Book I. without Vocabulary. 3d.
St. Matthew's and St. Luke's Gospels. 2s. 6d. each.
St. Mark's and St. John's Gospels. 1s. 6d. each.
The Acts of the Apostles. 2s. 6d.
St. Paul's Epistle to the Romans. 1s. 6d.

The Four Gospels in Greek, with Greek-English Lexicon. Edited by John T. White, D.D. Oxon. Square 32mo. price 5s.

WHITE'S GRAMMAR-SCHOOL LATIN TEXTS.

Cæsar, Gallic War, Books I. & II. V. & VI. 1s. each. Book I. without Vocabulary, 3d.
Cæsar, Gallic War, Books III. & IV. 9d. each.
Cæsar, Gallic War, Book VII. 1s. 6d.
Cicero, Cato Major (Old Age). 1s. 6d.
Cicero, Lælius (Friendship). 1s. 6d.
Eutropius, Roman History, Books I. & II. 1s. Books III. & IV. 1s.
Horace, Odes, Books I. II. & IV. 1s. each.
Horace, Odes, Book III. 1s. 6d.
Horace, Epodes and Carmen Seculare. 1s.

Nepos, Miltiades, Simon, Pausanias, Aristides. 9d.
Ovid, Selections from Epistles and Fasti. 1s.
Ovid, Select Myths from Metamorphoses. 9d.
Phædrus, Select Easy Fables.
Phædrus, Fables, Books I. & II. 1s.
Sallust, Bellum Catilinarium. 1s. 6d.
Virgil, Georgics, Book IV. 1s.
Virgil, Æneid, Books I. to VI. 1s. each. Book I. without Vocabulary, 3d.
Virgil, Æneid, Books VII. to XII. 1s. 6d. each.

LONGMANS, GREEN, & CO., London and New York.

THE FRENCH LANGUAGE.

Albitès's How to Speak French. Fcp. 8vo. 5s. 6d.
— Instantaneous French Exercises. Fcp. 2s. Key, 2s.
Cassal's French Genders. Crown 8vo. 3s. 6d.
Cassal & Karcher's Graduated French Translation Book. Part I. 3s. 6d.
    Part II. 5s. Key to Part I. by Professor Cassal, price 5s.
Contanseau's Practical French and English Dictionary. Post 8vo. 3s. 6d.
    — Pocket French and English Dictionary. Square 18mo. 1s. 6d.
    — Premières Lectures. 12mo. 2s. 6d.
    — First Step in French. 12mo. 2s. 6d. Key, 3s.
    — French Accidence. 12mo. 2s. 6d.
    — — Grammar. 12mo. 4s. Key, 3s.
Contanseau's Middle-Class French Course. Fcp. 8vo. :—
    Accidence, 8d.
    Syntax, 8d.
    French Conversation-Book, 8d.
    First French Exercise-Book, 8d.
    Second French Exercise-Book, 8d.
    French Translation-Book, 8d.
    Easy French Delectus, 8d.
    First French Reader, 8d.
    Second French Reader, 8d.
    French and English Dialogues, 8d.
Contanseau's Guide to French Translation. 12mo. 3s. 6d. Key 3s. 6d.
    — Prosateurs et Poètes Français. 12mo. 5s.
    — Précis de la Littérature Française. 12mo. 3s. 6d.
    — Abrégé de l'Histoire de France. 12mo. 2s. 6d.
Féval's Chouans et Bleus, with Notes by C. Sankey, M.A. Fcp. 8vo. 2s. 6d.
Jerram's Sentences for Translation into French. Cr. 8vo. 1s. Key, 2s. 6d.
Prendergast's Mastery Series, French. 12mo. 2s. 6d.
Souvestre's Philosophe sous les Toits, by Stièvenard. Square 18mo. 1s. 6d.
Stepping-Stone to French Pronunciation. 18mo. 1s.
Stièvenard's Lectures Françaises from Modern Authors. 12mo. 4s. 6d.
    — Rules and Exercises on the French Language. 12mo. 3s. 6d.
Tarver's Eton French Grammar. 12mo. 6s. 6d.

THE GERMAN LANGUAGE.

Blackley's Practical German and English Dictionary. Post 8vo. 3s. 6d.
Buchheim's German Poetry, for Repetition. 18mo. 1s. 6d.
Collis's Card of German Irregular Verbs. 8vo. 2s.
Fischer-Fischart's Elementary German Grammar. Fcp. 8vo. 2s. 6d.
Just's German Grammar. 12mo. 1s. 6d.
— German Reading Book. 12mo. 3s. 6d.
Longman's Pocket German and English Dictionary. Square 18mo. 2s. 6d.
Naftel's Elementary German Course for Public Schools. Fcp. 8vo.
    German Accidence. 9d.
    German Syntax. 9d.
    First German Exercise-Book. 9d.
    Second German Exercise-Book. 9d.
    German Prose Composition Book. 8d.
    First German Reader. 9d.
    Second German Reader. 9d.
Prendergast's Mastery Series, German. 12mo. 2s. 6d.
Quick's Essentials of German. Crown 8vo. 3s. 6d.
Selss's School Edition of Goethe's Faust. Crown 8vo. 5s.
    — Outline of German Literature. Crown 8vo. 4s. 6d.
Wirth's German Chit-Chat. Crown 8vo. 2s. 6d.

LONGMANS, GREEN, & CO., London and New York.

www.ingramcontent.com/pod-product-compliance
Lightning Source LLC
Chambersburg PA
CBHW031752230426
43669CB00007B/590